Production of Presence:
What Meaning Cannot Convey

Production of Presence

What Meaning Cannot Convey

Hans Ulrich Gumbrecht

STANFORD UNIVERSITY PRESS

STANFORD, CALIFORNIA 2004

Stanford University Press
Stanford, California
© 2004 by the Board of Trustees of the
Leland Stanford Junior University
Printed in the United States of America

Library of Congress Cataloging-in-Publication Data

Gumbrecht, Hans Ulrich.
    Production of presence : what meaning cannot convey /
Hans Ulrich Gumbrecht.
        p.   cm.
    Includes bibliographical references and index.
    ISBN 0-8047-4915-9 (cloth : alk. paper) —
    ISBN 0-8047-4916-7 (pbk : alk. paper)

        1. Aesthetics.   2. Experience.   I. Title.

BH301.E8 g86   2004
121'.68—dc21   2003021086

This book is printed on acid-free, archival-quality paper.

Original printing 2004

Last figure below indicates year of this printing:
13   12   11   10   09   08   07   06   05   04

Designed and typeset at Stanford University Press in 11/15 Garamond

This book is dedicated to

LAURA TERESA

whose presence tells me that I am alive,

every morning—

Acknowledgments

Perhaps more than any other clan of academics, scholars in the Humanities indulge in complaining about the institutional aspects of their working conditions. I have no ambition to be recognized as an exception to this venerable rule—but I would like to add today, very gratefully and very fondly, that working on this book gave me the conviction of living in the best of all possible intellectual worlds, both at Stanford University and in the larger Republic of Letters. So many colleagues and friends indeed actively helped me in thinking through, in writing, and even in revising my small book that, for banal reasons of space and proportion, I shall only be able to acknowledge those whose support was very specific and palpable (many others are mentioned and quoted in those chapters that fall under the generic definition of being a "generational fable"). I shall divide the addressees of my gratitude into two groups, one at Stanford and one in the Republic of Letters at large—and I cannot even remember all those who, with extreme (and I fear: poorly rewarded) patience were listening over more than a decade to earlier versions of my ideas on "materialities," followed by the "non-hermeneutic," followed by "presence."

At Stanford, I want to thank, above all, Joshua Landy, Matthew Tiews, and Margaret Tompkins, without whose insistence (differently motivated in each of their cases) I would have simply given up on this book. I am equally grateful to Robert Harrison, for I can no longer imagine my intellectual life without his presence; to Keith Baker, for thinking that writing is what I should mainly do (I wish he were right); to John Bender, for breakfasts at Printer's Inc.; to Robert Buch, for the exquisite politeness of being interested in my manuscripts and offprints; to Bliss Carnochan, for feeling an agenda (that I cannot spell out here) through the wall that separates our library carrels; to Niklas Damiris, for alienatingly exciting reactions (or was it meant to be a spanking?); to Charlotte Fonrobert, for drawing a line between theology and a "religious thinker"; to Cary Howie, for being the first who read this as a book; to Trina Marmarelli, for being so graceful (and such a genius reader too); to Aldo Mazzucchelli, for convincing me that even semiotics can be about presence; to Gabrielle Moyer, for accepting that the absence of meaning is not necessarily meaningless; to Andrea Nightingale, for the compliment of trying to talk me out of academic writing; to Nico Pethes, for remembering *Materialität*; to Norris Pope, who showed even more patience than some of my other friends; to Darlene Reddaway, for her benign but never condescending smile on academic life; to Tom Sheehan, for calling my Heidegger "earthy."

From two different (and not only geographically opposite) Atlantic shores Miguel Tamen and João Cézar de Castro Rocha have accompanied and fostered the protracted childhood and adolescence of this book with a presence and an intellectual sharpness that no real presence could have outmatched. My thanks also go out to Henning Ritter at Frankfurt on whose (more than) approval I would never have dared to count when I started writing; to Luiz Costa Lima at Rio de Janeiro, for a scary moment in a heated discussion; to Hermann Dötsch at Munich, for the very hard times (live and epistolary) that he gave me; to Valentín Ferdinán, at Middlebury and Montevideo, for his most heartfelt intentions to read; to Werner Hamacher at Frankfurt, for bringing up problems that I had not seen; to José Luis Jobim at Rio de Janeiro, for his tongue-in-cheek kind of a blessing; to Ulla Link-Heer at Hattingen (and at several other places), for never getting tired; to Valdei Lopes de Araújo at Rio de Janeiro, for his quiet enthusiasm; to Alfonso Mendiola at Mexico City, for the longest of all conversations; to Felicitas Nöske at Hamburg, for never letting me pass like a train in the night; to Catherine Pickstock at Cambridge, for the only electronic mail that has ever deserved to be called "beautiful"; to Joan Ramón Resina at Cornell, for so kindly overestimating me; to Mads Rosendahl at Copenhagen, for his intense *Gelassenheit*; to Violeta Sánchez Lorbach at Berlin, for agreeing to be the godmother; to Thomas Schleich at Elsfleth, for the gift of a piercing; to Tony Stephens at Sydney, for not liking my "parenthetic" style; to Bernd Stiegler at Frankfurt, for never getting enough; to David Wellbery at Chicago, for the (sometimes nagging) question about being a "religious thinker"; and to Guillermo (y Pilar de) Zermeño at Mexico City, for an unforgettable octopus.

Contents

User's Manual

This short book uses a number of more or less "philosophical" concepts in an unfamiliar way. But it needs so many pages to explain why it does so that it would not be far from the truth to say that the ongoing explanation and complexification of concepts is the book's main purpose. In order to avoid misunderstandings and the subsequent readerly frustrations right from the start, some initial—and very elementary—definitions might be useful. The word "presence" does not refer (at least does not mainly refer) to a temporal but to a spatial relationship to the world and its objects. Something that is "present" is supposed to be tangible for human hands, which implies that, conversely, it can have an immediate impact on human bodies. "Production," then, is used according to the meaning of its etymological root (i.e., Latin *producere*) that refers to the act of "bringing forth" an object in space. The word "production" is not associated here with the manufacturing of artifacts or of industrial merchandise. Therefore, "production of presence" points to all kinds of events and processes in which the impact that "present" objects have on human bodies is being initiated or intensified. All objects available in "presence" will be called the "things of the world." Although it is possible to claim that no worldly object can ever be available, in an unmediated way, to human bodies and human minds, the concept "things of the world" does include, as a connotation, a reference to the desire for such immediacy. There is no need to consult linguistic or philosophical handbooks in order to understand the meaning of the word "meaning" (and of "attribution of meaning") in the subtitle and throughout the chapters of this book. If we attribute a meaning to a thing that is present, that is, if we form an idea of what this thing may be in relation to us, we seem to attenuate, inevitably, the impact that this thing can have on our bodies and our senses. It is in this sense, too, that the word "metaphysics" is used here. In contrast, and although a number of theological concepts and motifs are discussed throughout the following chapters, those meanings of "metaphysics" that are synonymous with "transcendence" or "religion" have been avoided. "Metaphysics" refers to an attitude, both an everyday attitude and an academic perspective, that gives a higher value to the meaning of phenomena than to their material presence; the word thus points to a worldview that always wants to go "beyond" (or "below") that which is "physical." Different in that from "presence," from "production," and from the "things of the world," the word "metaphysics" plays the role of a scapegoat in the little conceptual drama of this book. "Metaphysics" shares this scapegoat position with other concepts and names, such as "hermeneutics," "Cartesian worldview," "subject/ object paradigm" and, above all, "interpretation." While such conceptual role distributions imply a risk of turning quite obsessive, it should be understood that the book's emphasis on "presence," "production," and "things of the world" does not go as far as to condemn any modes of a meaning-based relationship to the world.

STAKES

This book seeks to make a pledge against the tendency in contemporary culture to abandon and even forget the possibility of a presence-based relationship to the world. More specifically: to make a pledge against the systematic bracketing of presence, and against the uncontested centrality of interpretation, in the academic disciplines that we call "the humanities and arts." While modern (including contemporary) Western culture can be described as a process of progressive abandonment and forgetting of presence, some of the "special effects" produced today by the most advanced communication technologies may turn out to be instrumental in reawakening a desire for presence. The saturation of such a desire, however, cannot happen through a simple replacement of meaning with presence. What this book ultimately argues for is a relation to the things of the world that could oscillate between presence effects and meaning effects. Presence effects, however, exclusively appeal to the senses. Therefore, the reactions that they provoke have nothing to do with *Einfühlung*, that is, with imagining what is going on in another person's psyche.

AFFINITIES

There is no single academic "school" or "school of thought" to which the content of this book belongs. It certainly does not adhere to the European tradition of "hermeneutics" (on the contrary!), nor is it an exercise in "deconstruction," and it is at an even larger distance from "cultural studies" or (God forbid!) "Marxism." No special claims for ethically meritorious values such as "irreverence," "resistance," or "independence" are made, however. For this book owes more than it can possibly express to the ideas provoked by the work of two much admired friends and colleagues. Its five chapters mark a trajectory inspired, since the 1980s, by Friedrich Kittler's discovery of a new *sensibilité intellectuelle* for all kinds of "materialities." This trajectory has,

however, been gently derailed and very subtly reset for me by
Robert Harrison's unique style of dealing with some classic issues
of philosophical existentialism, among them the importance of
space, of the earth, and of the dead for human life. In addition,
the third chapter ("Beyond Meaning") offers an account of some
more punctual affinities between this reflection on "presence"
and a number of recent books from different disciplines within
the humanities. But these multiple affinities do not converge in
the promise (or threat) of a new intellectual position or a new
academic paradigm. Finally, while the author admits that it has
become difficult for him to imagine his own work without the
philosophy of Martin Heidegger, the last thing that he would be
willing to accept is the label "Heideggerean." His reasons for this
refusal are not philosophical reasons.

TONES

Some readers of this book's original manuscript noticed a strange
alteration between surprisingly (not to say outrageously) "auto-
biographical" tones in the first and last chapters and a more academic style in the intervening ones. Others found the manuscript unacceptably self-centered altogether—which, given the
scandalous number of books and articles of his own that the
author refers to in the footnotes, is a criticism that he cannot
easily reject. The author therefore feels obliged to admit that he
does not have any good excuse (but is there ever a "good" excuse
anyway?), let alone convincing reasons, for the way in which this
book expresses itself. Sure enough, he partly felt compelled to
write in such a specific way because he thought it was necessary
to find a specific place for his very personal pledge (and for the
way in which this pledge had emerged) in an intellectual space
with strangely blurred contours. But the author never made a

decision for or a choice of the book's discursive alterations. Perhaps, however, these alterations are not merely a personal and individual reaction to an intellectual environment in which long-valid certainties and positions and schools are fading, while no new certainties and positions and schools seem to appear at the horizon. As one of the author's more insightful (and very generous) friends recently suggested: under such circumstances, we cannot help being our own intellectual environment, and we even have to be the frames of reference for the work we are interested in.

REPETITIONS AND STRUCTURE

Some intellectual motifs, some quotations, some arguments, and even some definitions surface several times in the following chapters—as if they were a poorly edited collection of essays made into the semblance of a book, and not what they really are, namely, a book written, from the first to last page, in one stretch of sustained concentration. The reason for so many repetitions must be that the book's first impulse came as an intense intuition (and it remained an intuition throughout), rather than in the sequential shape of an argument. The author has done his best to transform this intuition about "presence" into a conventional narrative (a friend and reader said into a "generational fable") that starts in the past, culminates in the present, and ends with a view into possible futures. Despite this narrative surface, however, the intellectual movement that the author went through felt like a movement of complexification in concentric circles. This is why, at some point, he gave up his valiant fight against repetition—and this is also why he now hopes that these repetitions may work as pacemakers for future readers.

Production of Presence:
What Meaning Cannot Convey

Materialities / The Nonhermeneutic / Presence: An Anecdotal Account of Epistemological Shifts

1

Perhaps one can call the claim of this book "anticlimactic"—but if this were an adequate word at all, the anticlimactic claim would certainly not go as far as some friends from my generation may wish it did. It would not imply that everything anticlimactic is also "revolutionary" (in an intellectual or in a political sense). In a time when, not without reasons (some of them even good reasons), many scholars and most of the students in the humanities have become weary of "theory," that is, of a type of abstract thinking, often imported from or inspired by philosophy, whose "application" we used to think could energize our teaching and writing—in a time when we have become tired of "theory," this book will suggest that a certain "theoretical" move could indeed reenergize our dealings with all kinds of cultural artifacts and maybe even enable us to reconnect with some phenomena of our present-day culture that now seem to be out of reach for the humanities. The shortest way of announcing how I shall try to argue this claim is to say that the book will challenge a broadly institutionalized tradition according to which interpretation, that is, the identification and/or attribution of meaning, is the core practice, the exclusive core practice indeed, of the humanities. Concepts like "materiality," the "nonhermeneutic," "presence," and others will stand both for this challenge against the universality claim of interpretation—but also for scholarly practices that would be complementary to interpretation. Without trying to escape its anticlimactic stance, "epistemological" would probably be a more appropriate adjective than "theoretical" to characterize this book's dominant level of argumentation. For it pledges for a rethinking and, ultimately, for a reconfiguration of some of the conditions of knowledge production within the humanities, rather than producing new positive knowledge or revising traditional knowledge. Challenging the exclusive status of interpretation within the humanities, however, does not mean that this book is "against interpretation." It is interested in what it will suggest we think and, as far as possible, describe as "presence" but it by no means aims at being antihermeneutic. In this spirit, the book will suggest, for example, that we conceive of aesthetic experience as an oscillation (and sometimes as an interference) between "presence effects" and "meaning effects."

Being thus both future-oriented (which, strangely somehow, may seem old-fashioned today) and being embedded in an awareness of its anticlimactic gesture (which is a random result rather than a deliberate strategy: I simply wrote this much later than I should have), my book will lead you back into the intellectual past, several times, with the goal of laying open—on very different levels and with different intentions—"where it comes from." The retrospective view of this opening chapter is chronologically short and, almost necessarily, very personal. It tries to narrate the author's navigations, over the past twenty-five years roughly, on the lake (rather than on the ocean) of theory, and it does so for two reasons. One reason is that these navigations may be more or less typical of a generation of scholars who, today (for no other reason than their age—and for better or worse), dominate the scene in the humanities. At the same time (and this is the second reason for opening with a short retrospective), such a generational trajectory can be seen as part of a much larger and much longer-term epistemological shift, a shift whose narrative the second chapter seeks to recount. The second chapter begins with the emergence of early modern subjecthood and tries to argue that our present epistemological and cultural situation is overshadowed by an unresolved crisis that came up with a new form of world-observation in the middle of the nineteenth century. The short and anecdotal account of this introductory chapter, however, starts with a scene reminiscent of the famous "spirit of 1968"—a spirit that this book will make no attempt to revive—and it begins in a country that no longer exists.

For reasons that he has never quite understood (but they are of no importance anyway), the author and a Brazilian friend, who was then a visiting professor in Germany, had been invited to participate in a colloquium on "Functions of Fiction" (he cannot vouch for this title) at the Inter-University Center in Dubrovnik, Yugoslavia. While there was nothing outrageously bad about the week-long debates of this colloquium, what really impressed the two friends was the beauty and the liveliness of that Croatian city—an impression that they then quite desperately wanted to associate with Yugoslavia's official status as a socialist country. On the very early Sunday morning before their departure and after a long night on the beach, the two friends were watching the sunrise (unaware of how much this made them resemble Bouvard and Pécuchet). All of a sudden, the Brazilian friend, with the self-indulgent nostalgia proper to all cultures with Portuguese roots and with rather uncharacteristic loudness, began to express his regret over how unlikely it seemed that they would ever return to Dubrovnik. Wanting to be a good friend and very efficient, two ambitions whose Germanness he would then have flatly denied, the author (the German friend) almost immediately felt an obligation to resist such looming melancholia and decided to take the possibility of a return to Dubrovnik into his energetic academic hands. This was the reason why he was not even surprised—and immediately accepted—when, only a few weeks later, he received a letter from the director of the Inter-University Center inviting him to organize a colloquium there himself two years later. Today, he would say that there is no way to imagine this book without its Adriatic prehistory.

2

What the purpose (the "function," as we then preferred to say) of this colloquium should be was almost not a question back in 1979. The author felt (correctly) and regretted (with a spirit of urgency and of heroic resistance) that the impulses to reshape the humanities prompted by the famous year 1968, which were based on all kinds of leftist theories and political ideals, were now fast petering out. As one of the new interests that had emerged after 1968 was an interest in the history of the (academic) humanities, a symposium focusing on this topic and geared toward reenergizing the faltering theory and reform debates seemed to be (perhaps not the only, but certainly) an obvious choice. Thus began, in the spring of 1981, a series of colloquia, under the lofty rubrics "international" and "interdisciplinary," which would last until 1989, and which, he flatters himself today, made a certain impact on the author's generation of humanists in Germany.[1] As with any other project that one judges, in retrospect, "to have been successful," the Dubrovnik colloquia succeeded in a way that was quite different from the original intentions, and this both complicated and surprising "deviation" makes an interesting story about epistemological shifts.

The first three (of five) meetings all relied on one key assumption. It was, trivially and uncontestedly enough, the assumption that it was possible to learn from the past, and that this was, so to speak, particularly true for the history of the academic disciplines. We therefore explored the barely two centuries during which institutionalized literary studies and linguistics had existed three times and from many different angles in the hope of finding "orientations" for their future (most of us being literary scholars, we included linguistics in a spirit that was somehow close to a moral obligation: aware of the common origin of literary studies and of linguistics, we simply thought that we had no right to focus on literary studies alone). But while we felt encouraged both by the experience of how naturally some quite intense debates unfolded among the many academic disciplines that were represented and by an upbeatness that is typical, perhaps, at any given time of "the younger generation" in any profession, the palpable results of our search remained, frankly, disappointing. Yes, the history of literary studies and of linguistics turned out to be full of interesting and sometimes even moving episodes for us, who represented their present; but whatever we learned added up to the certainty that their past was too different from our present to ever contain any suggestions of a serious change in our convictions and practices. When we switched, for the second colloquium, from a general historical approach to the history of historical periodization in our disciplines and, for the third colloquium, to the critical uses that had been made of the concept of "style," we became affected, in addition, by a feeling

that one might call "the vertigo of constructivism." Banal as this
may sound today, we inevitably discovered—the hard way, or
perhaps it was the frustratingly soft way—that any kind of periodization was possible, of course; that the material from the past
of literature and language did not offer any "natural" resistance
to such narrative structures; and that, adding to the same disappointment, there was hardly any typological approach to the past
that could not be based on one or the other version of the concept of "style." Six years after the nostalgic sunrise on the beach
of Dubrovnik and three surprisingly successful volumes of "proceedings" later, we were, quite paradoxically, both disappointed
and encouraged enough to look for a decidedly different orientation in our discussions.

The decisive intuition came in April 1985, on another Sunday
morning, when we were walking down Stradun, the marble-
paved street that runs through the old city of Dubrovnik. Rather
than continuing on our imagined path toward a possible intellectual future, the long detour through the histories of our disciplines, we were all immediately convinced (it was indeed like the
parody of a collective moment of conversion) when one of us
(the author tends to believe that it was Anton Kaes, who then, as
today, was teaching at Berkeley, but it might just as well have
been Karlheinz Barck, then from East Berlin and now from Berlin) more or less casually proposed the topic "materialities of
communication." This tentative title had a truly futuristic ring
to it. The word "communication" sounded promising because it
abandoned what we felt was too narrow and too traditional a focus of literary studies on "literature" (this was, after all, also a
time when many of us in literary studies had just given up the
hope that the century-long efforts to find a metahistorically and
transculturally viable notion of "literature" would ever lead to a

satisfying result). But, above all, both concepts, "communication" and "materialities," seemed to promise an alternative to the
endlessness of interpretation and of narrating the past in ever-
different ways. For although it was not clear at all what an alternative to the practice of interpretation might look like, we all
were—quite naïvely—longing for some resistance to the intellectual relativism that (some say almost inevitably) comes with
the culture of interpretation. Without thinking much about the
reasons for our weariness or asking whether there was really an
alternative (but simply not asking such questions is the strength
of moments of intellectual change), some of us wanted a more
sober culture of complex description as we saw it at work in the
sciences. We were also somewhere between cynically and naïvely
hopeful that the overwhelmingly obvious convergence between
"materialities" and "materialism" would, firstly, oblige us to be
faithful to Marxism (which almost all of us had embraced in
even more youthful years, and that some of us—with a very bad
conscience—had just begun to find less than convincing) and
that, secondly, this would allow our colleagues from several Eastern European countries—which then meant from the socialist
states—to return to Dubrovnik two years later. For in addition
to the beauty of the Dalmatian Adriatic, it was a strategical reason that had made us opt for Dubrovnik as the site of our colloquia: Yugoslavia was then probably the only country in Eastern
Europe that was completely open to scholars from the West, and
the other socialist states at least did not have a plausible ideologi-
cal reason to prevent members of their academic elites from going there.

The cover of the volume *Materialität der Kommunikation*,
which came out in 1988, displays the—somehow clumsy—key
definition for the colloquium on "Materialities of Communica-

tion" that indeed took place two years after that upbeat Sunday morning conversation on Stradun. "Materialities of communication," we ruled, "are all those phenomena and conditions that contribute to the production of meaning, without being meaning themselves." Now, although memories of one's youth tend to become too golden, the author maintains that if any one of the (more or less) academic meetings that he has attended deserves praise for having been "intellectually productive," in addition to "encouraging," "upbeat," "Dionysian," "carnivalesque" (in the best sense of this word, one still feels obliged to add, even after so many years), and perhaps even, quite ironically, "meaningful"—it is certainly "Materialities of Communication" in the spring of 1987. This at least was our collective euphoric impression. We all had the energizing and intoxicating feeling of being part of and contributing to a dramatic change, and it was only with the growing distance of our own retrospectives that we began to discover multiple affinities in our intellectual environment which, at least in part, explained to us our thematic choice and the intoxicating enthusiasm that it had produced.

There was in those days, for instance, a widespread enthusiasm for the level in Walter Benjamin's work that, rather than trying to be philosophical, celebrates the immediate physical "touch" of cultural objects (that this fascination was not yet clearly distinguished from Benjamin's attempts to embrace Marxism made it only more appealing to us). There was, in our much closer intellectual environment, the then still growing success of Friedrich Kittler's truly pathbreaking book *Aufschreibesysteme 1800/1900*, which offered both a "psychohistorical" thesis for the dominance of the paradigm of interpretation within the humanities *and* an alternative style of investigation, condensed in the concept of "psycho-physics." This style of investigation connected to the question of how intellectual movements were triggered by technological innovations and by their application in the invention of new communication media. There was also, as different from Kittler in his intellectual gestures as one could possibly imagine (which did not prevent both from developing a mutual intellectual fondness), the great medievalist Paul Zumthor, who had just abandoned the semiotic approach to literature that had made his work famous. Zumthor's attention was then shifting from semiotics' exclusive attention to structures of meaning to the development of a phenomenology of the voice and of writing as body-centered modes of communication. While Kittler and Zumthor participated in the colloquium on "Materialities of Communication," we also felt encouraged by the work of several philosophers who had not accepted our invitation to the Adriatic coast. Among them was Jean-François Lyotard, who, in 1985, had organized an exhibit under the title "Les Immatériaux" at the Centre Pompidou in Paris, built on the thesis that the electronic media revolution had initiated a fast-growing immaterialization—meaning, partly at least, a disembodiment—of human life. But we also wanted to see an intellectual ally in Jacques Derrida, who at the beginning of his philosophical trajectory (a good twenty years before our colloquium) had argued that the systematic bracketing of the "exteriority of the signifier" was one key reason for the devastating dominance, as we were quick to believe, of "logo-phono-centrism" in Western culture. In other words, not taking into account, for example, the materiality of the characters on wax, papyrus, or parchment was seen as the historical condition for the dominance of "meaning" and "spirit" in Western culture. Although we realized that they were more distant from the vague but conceptually congested center of our own enthusiasm than

Kittler, Zumthor, Lyotard, and even Derrida, we were also eager to discover affinities in the work of Michel Foucault and of Niklas Luhmann. For if from today's perspective, both Foucault's discourse analysis and Luhmann's systems theory present themselves as strongly meaning-based approaches to culture and society, we wanted to associate the ostentatious distance that they both took from any philosophical tradition centered on the concept of the subject with our own oedipal impulses against (rather than "critique of") a subject-centered culture of interpretation. Like everybody else in those years, we cherished suggestive (and highly metaphorical) concepts of self-description such as Foucault's famous image of the concept of "humankind" being a form drawn in the sand of a beach, his praise of the "positivity of facts" or of the "archive," and we admired (and often tried to imitate) the almost technological flavor that we found in Luhmann's writing.[2]

So much was clear—unsurprisingly clear, one might add with two decades of distance—that our (not so threateningly) oedipal revolt was indeed well protected and cushioned by the work of some of those scholars and philosophers from the preceding generations whom we most admired. Undoubtedly, interpretation was under general attack (Susan Sontag's famous essay "Against Interpretation" only seemed to confirm our own feeling)—at least as far as some of the traditional certainties about its procedures were concerned, at least in its exclusivity claim as the core practice of the humanities. This, of course, encouraged us to ask what other questions and approaches this exclusivity was excluding. Wilhelm Dilthey, whom the German tradition had surrounded with the aura of being a founding figure of the *Geisteswissenschaften*, that is, of that very conception of the humanities within which the dominance of interpretation had become official and programmatic in the early twentieth century, soon turned into the scapegoat of the in-group discourse that was fast taking shape among us. "Hermeneutics," the philosophical reflection on the conditions of interpretation that Dilthey had wanted to foster, became synonymous for us with "interpretation." Whenever we got carried away by our somehow oedipo-revolutionary spirit (after all, we still wanted to be the torchbearers of 1968), we had some vague intuition that—from a larger epistemological perspective—Dilthey's move might have been more reactive and more limiting than his admirers and his followers thought. We wanted to see him as an intellectual figure who, in his time, had mortgaged the future of the humanities with the sole purpose of keeping certain problems at bay. Of course, this was a typical conspiracy myth, and if it had any truth to it, its consequences would have only applied to the German situation—but a certain generational view of our intellectual past and present was doubtless beginning to emerge.

3

The prehistory of the academic enthronement of hermeneutics is, however, the topic of the following chapter. Back in the 1980s, the first reaction to our own enthusiasm remained much more "future-oriented" (as we would then have felt obliged to say). The move toward "materialities of communication" had opened our eyes to a multiplicity of fascinating topics that could be subsumed (at least approximately) under the concepts of "media history" and "body culture." Our main fascination came from the question of how different media—different "materialities"—of communication would affect the meaning that they carried. We no longer believed that a meaning complex could be kept separated from its mediality, that is, from the difference of

appearing on a printed page, on a computer screen, or in a voice
mail message. But we didn't quite know how to deal with this
interface of meaning and materiality. Different, therefore, from
many other scholars who, especially in Germany, immediately
directed their entire research efforts to those new topics, most of
us felt that we were not yet conceptually prepared to tackle them
in a more than metaphorical way. Secretly, we were quite happy
to blame, once again, hermeneutics for having reduced the conceptual and discursive range of our disciplines to what was re-
quired for the analysis of barely meaning-related phenomena. So
our next, forward-oriented step had to push, quite naturally, for
the development of concepts that would be able to grasp the
newly discovered topics. In choosing "Paradoxes, Dissonances,
and Breakdowns" as the title for the 1989 colloquium in Dubrovnik (which would bring the Yugoslavian series to an end), it
was our bet that a focus on historical cases and intellectual con-
stellations that—for a myriad reasons—had posed problems to
interpretation and meaning production in general, would yield at
least some initial elements for the development of an alternative—"nonhermeneutic," as we began to say—discourse. After
the 1989 colloquium, we had learned that thematizing such
limit-phenomena and limit-situations had not yielded any progress in our agenda of conceptual development. Case studies that
could test the limits of our concepts and epistemological premises were one thing; the dream of overcoming these was a very
different matter.

A few months after the fifth colloquium at Dubrovnik, the
author moved from his German university to a campus in north-
ern California. There, he received quite generous financial support
to organize yet another colloquium in this series, which took place
at Stanford University in April 1991 under the title "Writing/Ecri-

ture/Schrift." What we experienced of this meeting—and the disappointment was quite intense—was that we had lost the epistemological momentum that had inspired us in the mid 1980s.[3] For with the topic of "Writing," we got entangled in a then highly conventional debate about the philosophical foundations, the different varieties and, in our most iconoclastic moments, even the limitations of the deconstructive paradigm. As deconstruction, on the one hand, always insisted on the impossibility of positing stable structures of meaning and had long abandoned, on the other hand, its initial interest in the "exteriority of the signifier," we seemed to lose sight of the constellation of problems and interests that we had conquered under the heading "materialities of communication." At the same time, however, and largely unnoticed, a transformation of our basic questioning style occurred—perhaps under the impact of an intellectual environment in which the intention of shaping a new disciplinary program called "cultural studies" was becoming predominant. Cultural studies promised to describe and analyze cultural phenomena and cultural institutions, rather than assigning meaning to them. When, therefore, in 1993, the author wrote an epilogue for the English publication of a number of essays from the Materialities and Paradoxes volumes, he launched the thesis, for the first time, that the main interest in his intellectual environment had shifted from the identification of meaning (from "interpretation") to problems regarding the emergence of meaning, on both the historically specific and metahistorical levels.

4

Tentatively, the author called the new perspectives for research and reflection that seemed to open up through this shift away from interpretation the "nonhermeneutic field," which he tried

to structure around four poles that corresponded to his understanding of Louis Hjelmslev's concept of the "sign." Hjelmslev
combines the structuralist distinction between "signifier" and
"signified" (he refers to the signifier as "expression" and to the
signified as "content") with the Aristotelian distinction between
"substance" and "form." The four concepts that this combination yields are "substance of content" and "form of content," and
"substance of expression" and "form of expression." With "substance of content," Hjelmslev sought to refer to the contents of
the human mind before any structuring intervention (the concept is close to what we otherwise refer to as "imagination" or
"the imaginary"). "Form of content," in contrast, would not correspond to any spatial manifestation of meaning complexes but
exclusively to the contents of the human mind in well-structured
form (there is a clear affinity between this concept and Michel
Foucault's notion of the "discourse"). "Substance of expression"
would be those materials through which contents can be mani-
fested in space—but prior to their shaping into any structures:
thus paint (rather than color) would be substance of expression,
as would ink, or a computer as a technical array. "Form of expression," finally, would be the forms and colors covering a canvas, characters on a page (rather than ink), or the display on a
screen (rather than the computer as a machine).

The Hjelmslev quadrangle proved to be a good conceptual
tool for the identification of different research activities, different
theoretical positions, and their potential relationships. It made
us aware, for example, of a certain affinity between a then particularly intense philosophical reflection on the notion of the
"imaginary" and Derrida's deconstructive undermining of stable
meaning structures. It helped us understand (something that was
by no means generally accepted only ten years ago) that Fou-

cault's work was exclusively concerned with structures of meaning, without ever thematizing the human body or any other
phenomena that had to do with the form of expression (Foucault
himself had certainly never professed any interest in "materialities"). But above all, this structuring of the nonhermeneutic
field suggested a—very schematic—sequence of three questions
that would considerably complexify the first version of our one
question regarding the emergence of meaning. These three
questions thematized (1) the emergence of forms of content out
of substance of content, (2) the emergence of forms of expression
out of substance of expression, and, finally, (3) the coupling of
forms of content and forms of expression into signs or into larger
signifying structures—for example, into a written text, a speech,
or a pictogram.

5

Without any doubt (and especially in comparison to the intellectual depression caused by the 1991 colloquium on "Writing"),
as a structuring device, the nonhermeneutic field produced a
certain feeling of progress. At least, it produced the impression
that the impulse coming from the topic "materialities of communication" would not easily slip away. But it was also true,
unfortunately, that the triple question about the emergence of
meaning that the nonhermeneutic field had enabled us to formulate would only lead back, somehow inevitably, to a very conventional concept of the "sign" and of "meaning structures."
These concepts remain metaphysical, inasmuch as they continue
to presuppose that communication is predominantly about
meaning, about something spiritual that is carried by and needs
to be identified "beneath the purely material" surfaces of the
material. Secondly, the nonhermeneutic field would not help us

in developing new answers to the question that had been at the core of the "materialities of communication"-paradigm, that is, the (perhaps naïve) question of how (if at all) media and materialities of communication could have an impact on the meanings that they were carrying. Only this question, however, would transcend the dimension of the metaphysical, because only this question would abandon the all too neat separation of materiality from meaning.

At the same time, the author wants to state the obvious—once again: there is nothing intrinsically wrong with meaning production, meaning identification, and the metaphysical paradigm. What our modest academic rebellions tried to problematize was, rather, an *institutional* configuration within which the absolute dominance of meaning-related questions had long led to the abandonment of all other types of phenomena and questions. As a consequence of this situation, we saw ourselves confronted with a complete lack of concepts that would allow us to deal with what we called "materialities of communication."

If this anecdotal account of epistemological shifts within the humanities contains any true event, it occurred during a seminar that the author taught at the Universidade do Estado do Rio de Janeiro (UERJ) in the mid 1990s. He had barely arrived, in his lectures, at the—by then well integrated—narrative point of acknowledging his ignorance about the specific (not meaning-based) effects of materialities of communication when a student suggested, rather casually, that these effects could be described as "productions of presence." The Portuguese words *produções de presença* still resonate in the author's mind—but the unidentified student who had been the agent of what would become a true intellectual breakthrough for the author never returned to his class (a potential genius, this student probably didn't find it

worthwhile to take a seminar from somebody who had unsuc-
cessfully struggled for years with something that was plainly obvious to him).[4]

On the other hand, this very absence of its inventor gave the
author the opportunity to unfold the formula "production of
presence" with his own concepts and words. First and above all,
he wanted to understand the word "presence" in this context as a
spatial reference. What is "present" to us (very much in the sense
of the Latin form *prae-esse*) is in front of us, in reach of and tangible for our bodies. Likewise, the author wanted to use the word
"production" along the lines of its etymological meaning. If *producere* means, literally, "to bring forth," "to pull forth," then the
phrase "production of presence" would emphasize that the effect
of tangibility that comes from the materialities of communication is also an effect in constant movement. In other words, to
speak of "production of presence" implies that the (spatial) tangibility effect coming from the communication media is subjected, in space, to movements of greater or lesser proximity, and
of greater or lesser intensity. That any form of communication
implies such a production of presence, that any form of communication, through its material elements, will "touch" the bodies
of the persons who are communicating in specific and varying
ways may be a relatively trivial observation—but it is true nevertheless that this fact had been bracketed (if not—progressively—forgotten) by Western theory building ever since the
Cartesian *cogito* made the ontology of human existence depend
exclusively on the movements of the human mind. Conversely
and from an epistemological point of view, this also meant that
any philosophical and theoretical positions that are critical of the
Cartesian dismissal of the human body as *res extensa* and, with it,
critical of the elimination of space, can become potential sources

for the development of a reflection on presence.[5] Now, any viable
reflection on presence will have to break with the (now fading)
"postmodern" intellectual convention according to which all acceptable concepts and arguments have to be "antisubstantialist."
For a reflection on presence, in contrast, any conceptual tradition, beginning with Aristotle's philosophy, that deals with substance and space will be pertinent and unavoidable.

Once again, there is reason to emphasize that the rediscovery
of presence effects and the interest in "materialities of communication," the "nonhermeneutic," and "production of presence" by
no means eliminate the dimension of interpretation and meaning production. Poetry is perhaps the most powerful example of
the simultaneity of presence effects and meaning effects—for
even the most overpowering institutional dominance of the hermeneutic dimension could never fully repress the presence effects
of rhyme and alliteration, of verse and stanza. It is telling, however, that literary criticism has never been able to react to the
emphasis that poetry gives to such formal aspects—except for the
establishment of long, boring, and intellectually pointless "rep-
ertoires" that list, in chronological order, the different poetic
forms within different national literatures, and except for the so-
called "theory of over-determination," which claims, against all
immediate evidence, that poetic forms will always double and
reinforce already existing meaning structures. The intuition, in
contrast, that instead of being subordinated to meaning, poetic
forms might find themselves in a situation of tension, in a
structural form of oscillation with the dimension of meaning,
turned out to be another promising starting point toward a general reconceptualization of the relationship between effects of
meaning and effects of presence.[6]

6

It has already been noted, in passing, that the next chapter of this book presents a chronologically much deeper (and less personal) historical narrative that seeks to demonstrate how the anecdotal account of some epistemological shifts presented by this opening chapter is part of a larger development in the history of Western philosophy. This historical contextualization will lead to a thesis about the institutionalization of hermeneutics and interpretation as core components of the academic humanities. Starting with the third chapter, however, the book develops, on different levels, the motif of an intellectually and aesthetically productive tension between meaning effects and presence effects. Without making the case for a coherent "position" on the map of contemporary theories, the third chapter first discusses the work of several authors who, from very different perspectives, have contributed either to a critique of the universality claim of interpretation within the humanities or to the complexification of a nontemporal concept of presence. The book thereafter concentrates on Heidegger's notion of "Being," which is presented as the most inspiring philosophical resource available for a further development of reflection on presence. The third chapter ends with two tentative typologies. One of them proposes a binary distinction between "presence cultures" and "meaning cultures," presupposing that *all* cultures and cultural objects can be analyzed as configurations of both meaning effects and presence effects, although their different semantics of self-description often accentuate exclusively one or the other side. The second—nonbinary—typology presents, again based on the meaning/presence distinction, four different models of cultural appropriation. Both typologies are meant to exemplify how a stronger concentration on the presence component could enrich the analytical work within the humanities.

If the first two chapters offer two different but complementary versions of a prehistory of the present intellectual moment, and if the third chapter is at the center of this book because it opens a space for some of the conceptual work that corresponds to this present moment and its intellectual opportunities, the fourth chapter seeks to discuss possible consequences, within the humanities, of a reflection on presence. To explore such "futures," the chapter follows a very basic threefold division. Focusing on the concepts "epiphany," "presentification," and "deixis," it thematizes new, presence-based ways of thinking aesthetics; of reacting to our fascination with the past; and of dealing with our pedagogical obligations at the university. The section on teaching, in particular, addresses the—almost inevitable—question of what "social" and "political functions" (if any) a thus revamped (or, rather, rethought) practice in the humanities might fulfill. Finally, the fifth chapter returns to the issue of what the fascination with presence might possibly "yield," but tackles it from an existential rather than an institutional point of view, thus resuming the very personal, almost biographical tone of the first chapter, albeit without being its continuation or a response to it. On the contrary, asking myself why I am so taken with presence phenomena and by the possibility of thinking them through leads to an analysis of the present cultural situation in which, on a primary level, presence effects have so completely vanished that they now come back in the form of an intense desire for presence—one reinforced or even triggered by many of our contemporary communication media. Our contemporary fascination with presence—thus the concluding thesis of the book—is based on a longing for presence that in the contemporary context can only be satisfied in conditions of extreme temporal fragmentation.

Metaphysics: A Brief Prehistory
of What Is Now Changing

1

What quite a number of scholars and intellectuals of my generation have been reacting against is an epistemological configuration whose traces we can identify in our everyday languages with
surprising ease. That these traces and, through them, this epistemological configuration are always in our language and on our
minds is the reason why it is so difficult to escape from them and
to come up with plausible alternatives, at least in Western culture. The institutionally uncontested central position in the humanities of interpretation—that is, of the identification and of
the attribution of meaning—for example, is backed up by the
positive value that our languages quite automatically attach to
the dimension of "depth." If we call an observation "deep," we
intend to praise it for having given a new, more complex, particularly adequate meaning to a phenomenon. Whatever we
deem "superficial," in contrast, has to lack all these qualities, because we imply that it does not succeed in going "beyond" or
"under" the first impression produced by the phenomenon in
question (we normally do not imagine that anything or anybody
might desire to remain without depth). In both cases, we also
normally presuppose that the quality of observations and interpretations depends on the "adequate distance" that an observer is

able to take in relation to the phenomenon on which he focuses. Therefore, we must make a specific intellectual effort to realize how problematic it is to speak constantly of "the world" or of "the society" as if "world" and "society" were objects at a distance—in relation to which we can (or even must) occupy a position of remoteness.

Taking literally a word that has developed so many different meanings in its history that it is impossible to restrict it to just one definition, the convergence of such and other motifs into a configuration of presuppositions that is inherent in our everyday language can be called "everyday metaphysics."[1] We can then say that, in their institutionalized form, the humanities clearly have "metaphysical" implications. For both our everyday languages and what we sometimes call, a bit pretentiously, the "methods" of the humanities imply that it is an unconditionally good thing to go "beyond" ("meta-") what is purely "material" ("physics"). That we normally, as I said, do not question these premises in our everyday languages and in our scholarly work can, of course, be seen as the result—or, rather, as the sedimentation of multiple results—of several centuries of reflection on the structures of knowledge and on the conditions of knowledge production in Western culture. This very history, which we may (but need not) call a "history of Western metaphysics," is the subject of my second chapter.

Now, obviously, the history of Western metaphysics is a history of almost endless complexity and a history, also, that has often been told, in its parts and in its entirety, by much more competent specialists than myself. If I venture to tell it again, I need to say why this history is so important for the point that I want to make in this book—which should also yield some clarity as to those questions and details, within this history, that I am specifically interested in. One such question of specific interest is when and under which specific historical circumstances interpretation and its metaphysical underpinnings became as central and as unquestionably important for the humanities as a cluster of academic disciplines as they have been until the present day. Secondly, it needs to be explained why, over the past thirty years, there has been, among many humanists at least, a feeling of discontent in reaction to this epistemological and disciplinary disposition (although these discontented humanists are far from being a majority among their colleagues). In other words: if the story told in the first chapter is that of subsequent—recent— reactions to the metaphysical implications of the humanities, how are we to explain why this "resistance" did not arise earlier—and why did it arise at all? Finally, we can of course hope that finding answers to these two questions will help us to decide whether it is desirable at all to overcome the exclusive and central status of interpretation within the humanities—and, if the answer should be affirmative at all, it will also help us to imagine how we might go about it.

2

Like the history of any philosophical motif, the story that I want to tell concerns changing forms of human self-reference. I mention this because connecting such forms and motifs of human self-reference to the names of different historical periods seems almost unavoidably to produce the danger of a specific misunderstanding. This misunderstanding would be the impression that the concepts in question refer to changes in the "reality" of human life, rather than to transformations in the concepts of self-description. "Renaissance" and "Early Modernity," the two names that we use for the period with which I shall begin my

narrative, are a particularly rich example of the divergence between a dominant cultural self-reference and our historical retrospective on the "reality" of that very same culture.

There was a certain iconographic tradition in those centuries
that still showed the world as a flat surface on top of which the
spheres rose like a dome. Such scenes are necessarily presented as
if perceived from an outside perspective. Sometimes we even see,
seemingly from outside, an allegorical figure representing humankind who breaks through the spheres as if he wanted to join
us. This double innovation (i.e., man being an outside observer
of the world and man being seen in this position) is a symptom
of a new configuration of self-reference in which men began to
see themselves as eccentric to the world, and this position was
different from the dominant self-reference of the Christian Middle Ages, when man understood himself as part of and as surrounded by a world that was considered to be the result of God's
Creation. A second change in comparison to the Middle Ages
lies in the implication (whose consequences would be conceptually unfolded only centuries later) that this human figure in its
eccentricity vis-à-vis the world is a purely intellectual, disembodied entity. It can afford, so to speak, to be a purely intellectual entity because the only function to which it is explicitly assigned is that of being an observer of the world, for which function exclusively cognitive faculties seem to be sufficient. Of
course, a self-reference that insists on its own bodylessness will
also claim, whenever challenged on this behalf, that is cannot be
gender-biased—which had indeed become an important element
of modern epistemology by the seventeenth century (although
feminist philosophy has recently and quite convincingly argued
that the claim of being "genderless" served as a shield protecting
the strong male bias of modern epistemology). At any event, the

world that the observer observed and interpreted was supposed to be purely material. Of course, this dichotomization between "spiritual" and "material" is the origin of an epistemological structure on which Western philosophy would from now on rely as the "subject/object paradigm." Its very elementary binary logic attributes the human body to the side of the objects of the world whereas, in medieval thought, spirit and matter were believed to be inseparable, both in human beings and in all the other elements of the divine Creation. The expectation and the iconography of a bodily resurrection of the dead on doomsday, for example, made this implication of medieval epistemology visible, as did the cultural premise that art historians have come to call "symbolic realism." In symbolic realism, each of the objects that make up the world has its inherent meaning, given to it by God in the act of Creation (this exactly was the key presupposition of some textual genres as obsessively cultivated during the Middle Ages as the so called "lapidaries" and "bestiaries"—where the meanings and sometimes even the magical qualities proper to different types of stones and different species of animals were meticulously explained). Interestingly (and typically), it was only toward the end of the Middle Ages, in a time when its basic epistemological features began to lose their appearance of being "natural," that such implications were increasingly made explicit.[2]

For the new type self-reference that posits that humans are eccentric to the world, however, this world is primarily—and perhaps we might even say exclusively—a material surface to be interpreted. To interpret the world means to go beyond its material surface or to penetrate that surface in order to identify a meaning (i.e., something spiritual) that is supposed to lie behind or beneath it. Conversely, it also becomes more and more conventional to think of the world of objects and of the human body as surfaces that "express" deeper meanings. Indeed, the paradigm of expression (chronologically) emerges with and (systematically) belongs to the same epistemological context as the paradigm of interpretation.[3] World-interpretation begins to be understood as an active production of knowledge about the world: it is mainly seen as "extracting inherent meanings" from the objects of the world—and in this aspect lies the decisive step toward modernity. For the assumption that the phenomena have their inherent meanings would not yet change on the threshold between medieval and early modern culture (interpretation would not be understood, broadly, as an attribution rather than as an identification of meaning until the nineteenth century). But humankind had never during the medieval centuries conceived of itself as actively producing knowledge. Knowledge about the details and about the overarching features of God's Creation was thought to be only available through divine revelation (or it was thought to be withheld, by God, from human insight), which, of course, was imagined to be independent of any human desire or need. This may explain why medieval culture was so obsessed with the threat and with the fear of losing knowledge. It is probably no exaggeration indeed to say that fighting this threat was the strongest of all motivations that carried the intellectual culture of the Middle Ages.

Only with the subject slowly establishing itself as an active role that implies the capacity and the right of producing new knowledge did the idea of accumulating and thus ultimately extending the amount of knowledge available to humans become thinkable and appealing. In tandem with this new self-attribution, however, agency (i.e., the idea of humans wanting and being able to change and transform the world) would appear. Until then, changes perceived in the world had been routinely seen as the consequence of morally illegitimate—but normally not fully conscious or deliberate—human interventions in the divine order (*mutabilitas*, i.e., "human fickleness" was the concept in question here) or as God's just punishment thereof. Finally, a subject that believes that it can produce knowledge will also feel able to hide and to manipulate knowledge. Significantly enough, in this sense, medieval culture had only acknowledged the harsh distinction between truth and lie; it had never developed concepts corresponding to our understanding of "fiction" or of "feigning." The evilness of the pagans in the *Song of Roland* is thus inscribed upon their bodies. But this also is why Chrétien de Troyes has such a hard time explaining that the fairy tales (he calls them "tales of folly") that he uses to establish the plots of his romances are capable of conveying moral truths. This also finally explains why early moderns reflecting on rhetoric and strategies of government were so fascinated with different techniques of manipulation. Machiavelli called Fernando of Aragón the most capable ruler of his time because he thought him capable of feigning, that is, of "covering his intentions and plans," as Machiavelli says, "under the mantle of pretended religious motivations." The origin of a modern concept of "ideology" can easily be seen here.

Very schematically, we may then describe this new, early modern view in which Western culture begins, over several centuries, to redefine the relation between humankind and the world as the intersection of two axes. There is a horizontal axis that opposes the subject as an eccentric, disembodied observer and the world as an assembly of purely material objects, including the human body. The vertical axis then stands for the act of world-interpretation through which the subject penetrates the surface of the world in order to extract knowledge and truth as its underlying meanings. I propose to call this worldview the "hermeneutic field." Of course, I know that it was only centuries later that "Hermeneutics" became the name of the philosophical subfield that concentrates on the techniques and the conditions of interpretation.[4] But long before the emergence of this academic subdiscipline, "interpretation" (and, with it, "expression") had become the predominant—and, soon afterward, the exclusive—paradigm that Western culture made available for those who wanted to think the relationship of humans to their world.

3

Of course, there is an infinity of cultural situations and of cultural phenomena that can illustrate this transition from medieval cosmology to the subject/object paradigm and to the hermeneutic field as foundational for what we call (and are still used to as) the "modern world." Probably, none of those situations and phenomena is as central as the contrast and the transition between the medieval ("Catholic," if you like—although the word is, of course, anachronistic for the Middle Ages) and the Protestant (i.e., early modern) theology of the Eucharist.[5] For without any doubt, the sacrament of the Eucharist, that is, the production of God's Real Presence on earth and among humans, was the core ritual of medieval culture. Celebrating the mass was then, not just a commemoration of Christ's Last Supper with his disciples, but a ritual through which the "real" Last Supper and, above all, Christ's body and Christ's blood could "really" be made present again. The word "present" does not only, and not even primarily, refer to a temporal order here. It means above all that Christ's body and Christ's blood would become tangible as substances in the "forms" of bread and of wine. What shapes and explains this premodern understanding of the relationship between Christ's body and the bread, and between Christ's blood and the wine, is the Aristotelian concept of the sign—which is not based on the distinction, so familiar to us as part of the hermeneutic field, between a material signifier as surface and an immaterial meaning as depth. The Aristotelian sign, in contrast, brings together a substance (i.e., that which is present because it demands a space) and a form (i.e., that through which a substance becomes perceptible), aspects that include a conception of "meaning" unfamiliar to us.

The dichotomy between "material" and "immaterial" certainly does not hold for the Aristotelian concept of the sign. There is no "immaterial" meaning detached from a "material signifier." This is why the Latin words *hoc est enim corpus meum* ("for this is my body"), through which the transubstantiation—that is, the transformation of the substance of bread into the substance of Christ's body in the sacrament of the Eucharist and the deictic gestures that went along with it—were perfectly plausible to medieval culture. There was no problem with bread being the "form" that made the "substantial presence" of Christ's body perceptible. This also is why we might say, from an anthropological point of view, that the premodern and Catholic Eucharist functioned like an act of magic, an act through which a substance distant in time and space was made present. And it was precisely the presence of Christ's body and of Christ's blood as substances that became problematic in Protestant (that is, early modern) theology. Through intense theological discussions that lasted several decades, Protestant theology redefined the presence of Christ's body and blood into an evocation of Christ's body and blood as "meanings." Increasingly, therefore, the "is" in the sentence ". . . this is my body" must have been understood as "this signifies" or "this stands for" my body. The meanings of

Christ's body and Christ's blood would then evoke the event of the Last Supper—but they were not supposed to make the Last Supper present again. This new, Protestant understanding of the mass as an act of commemoration was first conceptualized by John Calvin. It was only now that the temporal distance that separated each individual mass from the Last Supper as its point of reference began to turn into an unbridgeable "historical distance," and here we begin to understand that a connection exists between the emerging, specifically modern conception of signification and the dimension of historicity—as a conquest of modernity. For in modern understanding, signs at least potentially leave the substances that they evoke at a temporal and spatial distance.

As the substance of Christ's body and the substance of Christ's blood were being replaced by body and blood as meanings in Protestant theology, so the attention of the spectators at theatrical performances switched from the actors' own bodies to the characters that they embodied.[6] What we have come to call a "character"—think of Shakespeare's Hamlet, for example, or of Racine's Phèdre—is a complex concept (normally a concept describing a complex psyche). As a specific concept, as a complex meaning, each character is progressively unfolded, together with other characters, through the plot of the drama. Modern theater still makes its plots available through the interaction of the actors' bodies and their voices on the stage. But as an innovation of early modern scenography, the curtain now separates the stage, where the plot is produced, from the space of the spectators. Thus the actors' bodies became removed (at least in theory) from the spectators' reach. In other words, whatever is tangible, whatever belongs to the materiality of the signifier, becomes secondary, and indeed removed from the early modern signifying scene, as soon as the meaning in question is being deciphered.

Most of medieval theater, in contrast, seems to have func-tioned in a very different way (if "theater" can be a precise enough word at all for a culture in which almost any act of communication was body-based performance). If we look at some of the medieval manuscripts that the philologists of the nineteenth and the early twentieth centuries labeled "theatrical" (not always for completely transparent reasons), we often discover that it is impossible to identify any narrative—that is, any progressive development of an action, let alone of characters. What these manuscripts focus upon, the situation for which they provide a choreography, is, on the one hand, the entry of an actor's (or a clown's or a joker's) body into a space that it will share with the bodies of the spectators. The joker will ask, for example, whether he is "allowed to come in," and after a supposedly affirmative answer from the crowd, he may ask again, adding that his presence will not be pleas-ant at all for the spectators. Inasmuch as the manuscripts very often provide no choreography for the subsequent interactions between the actors and the spectators, we must imagine that this—central—part was being improvised, depending on the components of each specific situation. What the manuscripts then again concentrate upon, on the other hand, is the exit or the farewell of the actors. In other words, the manuscripts provide a path for the undoing of the primary "theatrical" situation—in which the actors' bodies were not separated, by a curtain, from the bodies of the spectators, and in which it was clearly not the function of the actors' bodies to produce a complex meaning that the spectators were supposed to induc-tively decipher. The co-presence of actors and spectators in medieval culture seems to have been a "real" co-presence, in which mutual physical contact was by no means excluded—so little excluded indeed that the spectators of late medieval passion plays sometimes "executed" the body of the actor representing Christ, by throwing stones at him.[7]

Italian commedia dell'arte was perhaps the only staging convention that preserved similar presence effects within the cultural context of early modernity. The on-stage behavior of its different actors was roughly connected and coordinated, for each individual performance, through the choice of a narrative by the director of the group, a narrative within which the actors were supposed to play (but there was no joint script representing the plot of this narrative). The emphasis of commedia dell'arte lay, however, in the (often obscene) gestures that individual actors displayed in endless variations for their spectators (these types of theatrical gestures—"catching a fly," for example, or "crossing a forbidden threshold"—were called *lazzi*). The development of character concepts through the plot of a drama, in contrast, was not something that commedia dell'arte ever cared about. Its limited set of genre-specific roles remained stable throughout the entire history of this staging convention.

4

It is very interesting to see that during the seventeenth century, especially in Paris, the staging form of the commedia dell'arte (then called *la comédie des Italiens*) was competing with a new style of French theater that is best represented by the names of the three great classical French playwrights, Corneille, Molière, and Racine, in whose work the production of semantic complexity dominated the scene in the most overwhelming fashion—to the detriment of any presence effects. The actors in Corneille's or Racine's tragedies stood on the stage in a half-circle, reciting of-

ten highly abstract texts in the heavy verse form of the alexan-
drine. No Western theater style either before or afterward was
more "Cartesian" than French classical drama. Of course, I am
referring here to the proverbially famous reflection of Corneille's
and Racine's contemporary René Descartes, who for the first
time made the ontology of human existence, as *res cogitans*, explicitly and exclusively depend on the ability to think and who,
as a consequence, subordinated not only the human body but all
the things of the world as *res extensae* to the mind.

This may seem to suggest that I am saying that Descartes was
responsible for everything that went wrong, in a historical fan-
tasy about modern Western culture understood as persecution of
the body and repression of all presence effects attached to it. But
I am not really writing about Descartes's work in any specific
sense (and even less, of course, about Descartes's life).[8] Rather,
his name and the adjective "Cartesian" refer to the endpoint of a
century-long development on the level of *histoire des mentalités*, a
development that spans the earliest manifestations of Renaissance culture and the fully unfolded state of the hermeneutic
field. In the same historical context, the intense discussion about
the relationship between the cultural present of the seventeenth
century and the classical Greco-Roman age that took place in the
Académie française around 1700, which we today call the *Querelle des anciens et des modernes*, was one further step in the direction toward unfolding the multiple implications of the hermeneutic field. What I find so important about the *Querelle* is less
whether its different authors favored one or the other proto-form
within what would become a new style of "historical culture"
during the eighteenth and, above all, the nineteenth century.
The most elementary—and the most important—epistemological feature that events like the *Querelle* began to institutionalize

in modern Western culture was the priority of the dimension of time over that of space, in a culture that was no longer centered on a ritual of producing "real presence" but based on the predominance of the *cogito*—a predominance that had yet to crystallize into a ritual of its own.

The age of Enlightenment, then, was the time when human agency in the production of knowledge became a condition for knowledge to be acceptable, and when human agency as the claim, based on this critical revision of knowledge, to actively transform the world, began to shape the sphere of politics.[9] This was a further step—from many perspectives, the decisive step—in the unfolding of the implications of the hermeneutic field, which now really began to look like what we often refer to today as the "metaphysical worldview." Indeed, one might claim that the Enlightenment was the culminating moment of the metaphysical worldview because, on the one hand, it was now fully developed and, on the other hand, intrinsic problems and crises had not quite begun to interfere yet. Rather, the principle that all knowledge about the world should be knowledge produced by humans, had been taken so seriously since the beginning of the eighteenth century that all revealed knowledge, and all knowledge that had been acknowledged, for the same reason, as part of the tradition, was being subjected to a rigorous process of revision. The eagerness to collect this new knowledge and to put it into the broadest possible circulation made the eighteenth century the great age of dictionaries and encyclopedias.

No other age believed more profoundly in the power of knowledge. Those encyclopedias were being put together in the utopian expectation that, one day, knowledge about the world would be complete, and that this completed knowledge would be the basis for the creation of new social and political institutions, perfectly adapted to the needs of the human race. At the same time, however, the experience began to emerge that, although based on the most advanced knowledge as their shared orientation, individual plans about ways to produce these new institutions would not always and naturally converge. This is where a new idea of the public space and of politics started to develop. The public space was imagined as that sphere of deliberation where all participants would bracket their personal and group-specific interests in order to reach consensus. Such were the premises for the early institutions of political representation, above all, for the parliament as a place where the competition of different opinions and of different visions of the future was supposed to be transformed into consensus and into a joint punctual vision of the future. Perhaps we could go so far indeed as to say that, for the now fully unfolded metaphysical worldview, parliamentary politics became as central and as emblematic a ritual as the Eucharist had been for medieval culture. It was the competition between different minds and their different intentions, a competition that produced chesslike intellectual and rhetorical strategies.

For certain worldviews, the moments of their culmination coincide with the appearance of their first symptoms of crisis. More than ever before—and ever after—metaphysics (or the hermeneutic field) was firmly established as the dominant outline for human self-reference, and as the basis for any kind of collective practice in Europe, around the middle of the eighteenth century. But—at least in our retrospective—it is precisely then that the first cracks in the edifice of modernity appear. Seen from the history of Western philosophy during the nineteenth century, the work of Immanuel Kant, for example, appears as a unique monument in which the ambiguity of being simultaneously a culminating achievement of Enlightenment thought and a symptom of the beginning of the dissolution of the epistemology on which the Enlightenment was based found its emblematic expression. For the initial provocation of Kant's critical writing seems to have been the awareness of a distance between the subject and the world of objects, a distance that appeared wide enough to challenge the current philosophical assumption about modes of world-appropriation. But even those who hold that Kant was ultimately successful in eliminating this doubt, by showing that man's intellectual faculties were sufficient to grasp the world, will admit that his primary motivation came from the beginning of doubts about the viability of the subject/object paradigm.

The same problems are much more textually obvious in Diderot's and d'Alembert's *Encyclopédie*, another heroic enterprise of the age of Enlightenment. In their first (and never officially modified) conception for the secular effort of putting together all the available knowledge about the world that had been subjected to critical revision, the editors of the *Encyclopédie* relied on a double complementarity.[10] They were hoping that the contributions of different authors to individual entries of their *Dictionnaire raisonné* would always come together in univocal descriptions of the object or of the concept in question (tensions or contradictions were not expected). They also anticipated that the completion of their work would yield a clear outline (something like an "ontological floorplan") for all available knowledge, an outline that would exactly correspond to what they assumed to exist as a basic structure of the world of objects. In the publishing reality, however, many of their multiple-authored entries turned out to be contradicting or competing renditions of the objects and concepts that they thematized. At the same time, the editors' hope of identifying one (and only one) basic structure for the entire world of things and its representation through elements of knowledge was not even fulfilled in the very hypothetical *plan* that, as a folding sheet, preceded the first volume of the *Encyclopédie,* a confusing little map that distributes its items (i.e., the different fields of knowledge) on the surface of the page without any dominant principle of plausibility.

If knowledge thus turned out to be much more centrifugal than ever expected, the growing intellectual fascination with "materialist" thought and even the emergence of aesthetics, as a subfield of philosophy, in the eighteenth century, make it clear that, counter to the premises of the hermeneutic field, world-appropriation through the human body, that is, through the human senses, was now also reappearing as an epistemological option. Focusing on the novels of the Marquis de Sade, Michel Foucault has shown how, under these conditions of a beginning "crisis of representation," the activity of naming the things of the world was turning into a precarious and therefore obsessive enterprise.[11] This perspective, finally, opens up a new way of historical understanding on a series of texts and artworks that, toward the end of the eighteenth century, indulged in painting surprisingly skeptical pictures of the purely intellectual world-observer. For Jean-Jacques Rousseau's *promeneur solitaire,* the distance from the world is no longer just a mathematical condition that helps the production of valid knowledge; it now also begins to mark a sensitive soul's zone of retreat from a world that is increasingly perceived as aggressive. In *Le Rêve d'Alembert,* for example, Diderot describes his friend and co-editor, the mathematician d'Alembert, as shaken by a feverish delirium; and in one of the etchings of his *Caprichos,* Francisco de Goya created a new, emblematic view of the Enlightenment philosopher by de-

liberately playing with the semantic ambiguity of his famous leg-
end "El sueño de la razón produce monstruos," which means
both "the sleep of reason produces monsters" and "the dream of
reason produces monsters,"[12] thus simultaneously conventionally
praising and grotesquely debunking the powers of reason.

5

When the European societies emerged, during the second decade
of the nineteenth century, from almost thirty years of revolutions
and reforms that had started out with the hope of making true
what Enlightenment had promised them—that is, a new, collec-
tively happy order of life based on the perfection of human
knowledge—one thing was clear between all the competing
groups in the political and intellectual arena: the world was—at
least: the world was still—far behind the generous expectations
propagated by the generation of the "philosophers."[13] This also
was when multiple phenomena came together in reinforcing
those (at first) isolated symptoms of epistemological inconsis-
tency that we identified in the intellectual production of the late
eighteenth century—to finally provoke a thorough crisis of the
metaphysical worldview. For the description of this episte-
mologically decisive moment, I not only draw on *Les Mots et les
choses,* Michel Foucault's groundbreaking book on the *crise de la
représentation,* but use the distinction between "first-order observers" and "second-order observers" that Niklas Luhmann developed without ever thematizing the historical context of its origin.[14]

If the observer role that arose in early modernity as a key element of the hermeneutic field was merely concerned with finding the appropriate distance in relation to its objects, the second-
order observer, the new observer role that would shape the epis-

temology of the nineteenth century, was an observer con-
demned—rather than privileged—to observe himself in the act
of observation. The emergence of this self-reflexive loop in the
form of the second-order observer had two major consequences.
Firstly, the second-order observer realized that each element of
knowledge and each representation that he could ever produce
would necessarily depend on the specific angle of his observation.
He thus began to realize that there was an infinity of renditions
for each potential object of reference—which proliferation ultimately shattered the belief in stable objects of reference. At the
same time, the second-order observer rediscovered the human
body and, more specifically, the human senses as an integral part
of any world-observation. This other consequence coming from
the new observer role would not only end up problematizing the
pretended gender-neutrality of the disembodied first-order observer (this question can indeed be regarded as one of the origins
of feminist philosophy); above all, it brought up the question of
a possible compatibility between a world-appropriation by concepts (which I shall call "experience") and a world-observation
through the senses (which I shall call "perception").

Nineteenth-century philosophy and science were soon dominated by the formula of a—temporary—solution that intellectuals and scholars developed in reaction to the first of these two
challenges. In very abstract terms, we can characterize this solution as a switch from a mirrorlike style of world-representation,
in which each concept or one element of knowledge was supposed to correspond to a single phenomenon, to a style in which
each phenomenon would be identified through a narrative. I am,
of course, referring to the parallel discourses of (the Hegelian
type of) philosophy of history and to (the Darwinian type of)
evolutionism. How could the discursive structure of narration

turn into a solution for that problem within the crisis of representation that was triggered by the proliferation of possible representations for each phenomenon of reference? The answer lies in
the insight that narrative discourses open a space in which a
multiplicity of representations can be integrated and shaped into
a sequence. Together with philosophy of history and evolutionism, nineteenth-century literary "realism" was another discourse
that produced a plethora of reactions to the challenges of the new
multiperspectivalism in the view of the world.[15] Astonishingly,
perhaps, it was this discursive tradition that produced, in the
work of authors like Gustave Flaubert, the most pessimistic answers to the question of whether multiple worldviews could be
made to converge. The different perspectives that (for example)
Flaubert's protagonists are "embodying" never end up coming
together in a homogeneous view that would be their "world"—
and we know how hard Flaubert (and other authors of his time)
were working on this very effect.

The second epistemological problem stemming from the emergence of the second-order observer, the problem of the (non-)
compatibility of world-appropriation by concepts and world-
appropriation through the senses, did not even produce the illusion of a solution. All we can observe, between the nineteenth
century and our own intellectual present, is a never-ending series
of attempts, sometimes violent but never successful, at bringing
experience and perception together—and they converge with at
least one radical institutional move that tried to eliminate the
problem. Some of the earliest of these reactions can be subsumed
under the metaphor of a "sign-deregulation." By "sign-deregulation," I refer to several experiments that tried to modify the very
neat distinction, inherent in the hermeneutic field, between the
purely material surface of the signifier and the purely spiritual (or

conceptual) depth of the signified. The poets of the symbolist school, for example, among them Verlaine and Rimbaud, wanted to invest meanings, at least certain connotative meanings, into the sound structures of their texts. A poem like Mallarmé's "Un Coup de dé" seems to suggest that the layout of its words on the page can correspond to its meaning and to its potential sound. Richard Wagner's *Programm-Musik*, finally, set out to insert meaning into the sounds and rhythms of orchestral music.

During the final decades of the nineteenth century, philosophy, science, and literature abounded with other experiments dedicated to reconnecting experience and perception. It was thus the explicit goal of Émile Zola's series of twenty novels, *Les Rougon-Macquart*, to explain the history of several generations of a family through the convergence between its genetic disposition and the influence of multiple social environments.[16] Friedrich Nietzsche, who fascinated Heidegger as the last metaphysician (or as the first European philosopher to have overcome metaphysics), never stopped to praise the scholarly concentration on the philological surface values of texts and on the material superficiality of masks, thereby ridiculing all efforts to find ultimate meaning and truth below or behind them (read from this angle, Nietzsche is certainly postmetaphysical). Before laying the foundations of psychoanalysis as an exclusively interpretative method in his book *Traumdeutung* (*The Interpretation of Dreams*), published in 1900, Sigmund Freud had worked, for more than a decade, on several outlines that were meant to integrate the human psyche with human physiology. Finally, among many other thinkers of his time, Henri Bergson was convinced that the human memory was the one phenomenon whose conceptual dissection would lay open the connections between the mind and the brain.[17]

It is certainly telling that thinkers like Bergson, Freud, and
Nietzsche, who became unusually popular among the general
European readership around 1900 and whom, without any hesitation, many of us today count among our intellectual heroes,
struggled—mostly without success—for academic respectability
in their own time. For the official academic world was now
quickly moving toward radical solutions in reaction to the problem concerning the mediation between experience and perception, toward solutions that all ended up suggesting different
forms of separation between these two dimensions. On the epistemological level, one such solution was marked by Edward
Husserl's foundation of the philosophical style we call "phenomenology." In a polemical turn against the "naïve" belief of the
natural scientists that they could "grasp" the things of the world,
Husserl suggested (this at least is what many of his readers understood) that all objects outside the human mind were simply
inaccessible to us. This was one historical ending of the subject/
object paradigm, of the hermeneutic field, and of Western metaphysics. Phenomenological philosophy would soon concentrate,
exclusively, on the introspective efforts to describe those mechanisms through which the human mind itself produces ("con-
structs") views of the outside world. It thus became a matrix for
other contemporary styles or schools in philosophy (many of
them belonging to our present), which we characterize as
"constructivist"—on behalf of the general premise that whatever
they may analyze or deal with will be "constructions" (or projec-
tions) of the human mind.

A parallel institutional move took place at the University of
Berlin during the last decade of the nineteenth century.[18] It was,
above all, in the field of psychology that the epistemological in-
compatibility between perception and experience was now materi-

alizing in a fast-growing tension between, on the one hand, an experimental school of research, based on measurement and other scientific methods of investigation and, on the other, a philosophical approach that relied on the traditions and intuitions of understanding. In 1893, the philosopher Wilhelm Dilthey was successful in blocking the Berlin appointment of Hermann Ebbinghaus, an eminent representative of "scientific" psychology, whom he accused of "transgressions into the field of physiology." Exactly a decade later, Dilthey and fourteen of his colleagues proposed to the Ministry of Culture an institutional separation from all those scholars who were practicing such a scientific style of research. This (in the end successful) secession was the beginning of the institutional independence of the *Geisteswissenschaften* as a cluster of disciplines that, following Dilthey's programmatic proposal, was supposed to be centered around interpretation as its core practice and hermeneutics as its reflexive space. Once the methods of science and the dimension of perception were excluded from the *Geisteswissenschaften*, Dilthey believed, any kind of interpretation, above all literary and psychological interpretation, would ultimately uncover the immediacy of lived experience (*Erleben*) under layers of meaning. Thus, paradoxically, it was the crisis of metaphysics and of the hermeneutic field that provoked the enthronement of philosophical hermeneutics at the center of the *Geisteswissenschaften* as the newly shaped federation of the humanistic disciplines. The price that the humanities had to pay for this move was obvious: it was the loss of any non-Cartesian, any non-experience-based type of world-reference.

6

On multiple levels and in manifold contexts, therefore, the early twentieth century turned out a complex moment of intellectual departure within the newly shaped humanities—although not every nationally specific development was so emblematically clear as the events at Berlin. Motivated by the convergence between the wide-ranging (almost "popular") and enthusiastic reception of phenomenology all over Europe and the institutional influence of Dilthey and his school, the humanities concentrated, more than ever before, on the dimensions of meaning and on language as places and instruments of world construction. Here lie the beginnings of a type of cultural history and of sociology that, during the second half of the twentieth century, would focus on everyday worlds or on *mentalités* as "social constructions of reality."[19] This spirit of intellectual innovation also affected humanistic disciplines regarded as less central than philosophy or psychology. Throughout the nineteenth century, for example, literary scholarship had developed in two clearly diverging directions. Since its beginnings in early romanticism, the academic study of German literature had emphasized the importance of its chronologically earliest texts, whose analysis was expected to reveal the true essence of the German nation. While such an approach found at least some resonance, during the next hundred years, in all those European nations where, as in Germany during the age of romanticism, intellectuals deemed their fatherland to be in an intellectual or political crisis, a different style of literary scholarship emerged at many universities in Great Britain and the United States. Its dominant practice was a close reading geared toward ethical questions as well as toward moral instruction, and without paying any programmatic attention to questions of national origin or historical context. Faced with the epistemological, institutional, and, from World War I on, political challenges of the early twentieth century, "national philologies" tended to shed the concept of the nation as a disciplinary horizon, which had until then appeared to be an indispensable frame of reference for their historical research. In reaction to this loss, the 1920s became a productive age of experimentation for the national philologies, with new paradigms of transnational and intermediatic comparison, and with new, also transnational, concepts of historical periodization that would tentatively include art history, the history of music, and sometimes even political history or the soon emerging social histories. At the same time and under similar pressures, the Anglo-American style of literary reading developed a level of philosophical self-reflection—to which innovation its renaming as "new criticism" refers.[20] Without normally explicitly rejecting claims or at least implications of ethical validity, the new criticism certainly did not continue to occupy an institutional place that was mainly determined by the function of moral instruction. Those were the years, after all, when the literary authors of high modernism and the artists of the surrealist movement, reacting, it seems, to the frustration of their attempts to reconcile the dimensions of experience and perception, began to break loose, in multiple directions, from the principle of world-representation that had accompanied the rise of modernity.

But phenomenology, constructivism, and comparative cultural studies, new criticism and high modernism, in all their internal variety as intellectually "revolutionary" reactions and movements, made up only one of the two branches of reactions triggered by the long-term effects of the nineteenth century's epistemological crisis. This was the branch that, even today, we tend to call "progressive." The other sequence of reactions going back to the same origin was characterized by a feeling of loss and by a nostalgia, as its common denominator, for that reference to the world of objects in whose availability metaphysics had so

long and so strongly believed. During several decades, scholars
from many different fields pointed, with sometimes dramatic
gestures of complaint or regret, to the loss of (belief in) a world-
reference.[21] Analytic philosophy, in its institutional beginnings,
was eager to prove that at least a minimal degree of world-
reference could after all be achieved through language or, at least,
in carefully crafted elementary sentences. At the same time and
diverging, in their intellectual styles, as much from analytic philosophy as one can possibly imagine, wild thinkers and wildly
gesticulating artists, such as Georges Bataille and Antonin Artaud, accused Western culture of having lost touch with the human body.[22] While the optimism of Marxist scholars regarding
the pertinence of their analyses and insights remained strangely
(or suspiciously?) unperturbed in this environment of intensify-
ing epistemological skepticism, the intellectually most powerful
reactions to the loss—or, in this case, rather, to the fear of a
loss—of world-reference were those we call the "conservative
revolution," a term invented by the Austrian poet and playwright
Hugo von Hofmannsthal in the early 1920s.[23]

No other thinker, in this context, went further in criticizing
and in revising the metaphysical worldview than Martin Heidegger. Starting with the publication of his book *Sein und Zeit* in
1927, this effort gained him immediate international attention.
Heidegger replaced the subject/object paradigm with the new
concept of "being-in-the-world," which, so to speak, was supposed to bring human self-reference back in touch with the
things of the world (in this sense, "being-in-the-world" was a
reformulation, rather than a radical replacement of the sub-
ject/object paradigm). Against the Cartesian paradigm, he reaf-
firmed the bodily substantiality and the spatial dimensions of
human existence,[24] and he began to develop the idea of an "un-

concealment of Being" (in which context the word "Being" always refers to something substantial) as a replacement for the metaphysical concept of "truth" that points to a meaning or an idea. These indeed are some of the reasons why, even now, no attempt at overcoming metaphysics and its consequences can disregard Heidegger's work.

7

The national academic traditions and disciplines that succumbed to the promises of fascism or communism, and thus lost touch with the more advanced epistemological thinking of their time, will not be considered here. The one observation that interests me, however, and that is meant to connect the end of this chapter with the end of the previous chapter, refers to the decades following the end of World War II. I give this observation the condensed form of a thesis by saying that there were two parallel types of reaction to the loss of world-reference and of the dimension of perception during the first decades of the twentieth century: the various forms of constructivism, on the one hand, and the different attempts at bringing back reference and perception, on the other. The contrast and tension between them turned into an alternation between "soft" and "hard" intellectual styles within the humanities around 1950. Of course, there were all kinds of national and disciplinary developments to which such a broad statement cannot do justice. But I hold that, on the appropriate level of abstraction, this general observation is correct—and that it covers the experience of my own generation of scholars within the humanities, including the conclusion that no progress can be found in these movements of alternation between "hard" and "soft" paradigms.

In literary studies and in the neighboring disciplines, at least, the international success of the "soft" approach of new criticism and interpretative "immanentism,"[25] accompanied by a rise of literary hermeneutics, during the 1950s and the early 1960s can be partly explained as a reaction to different national episodes of political ideologization. It has been followed, however, since the late 1950s, by simultaneous waves of apparently "harder" paradigms.[26] Among them were the reception of structuralism, structural linguistics, and the so-called "Russian formalism" by literary studies. At least in their ambition to overcome the subjectivity of pure interpretation, these theories converged with a new enthusiasm for all kinds of sociological approaches, including different varieties of Marxism, and with the history of literary reception. It was only a decade later, in the 1970s and 1980s, that "postmodern" literary scholarship, under the "softening" influence of deconstruction and new historicism,[27] did what it could to make the preceding desire for theoretical and methodological rigor look as naïve as possible. Interestingly and despite their internal philosophical divergences, both deconstruction and new historicism started out with (differently argued) critiques of structuralism (i.e., of a "hard" paradigm), and they both found their most fertile reception among a generation of American literary scholars that had been brought up in the interpretative style of new criticism.

There is no doubt that the first three of the Dubrovnik colloquia referred to in the previous chapter can be explained, from our present-day retrospective, as trying to explore the possibilities of a broadly understood neohistorical praxis. It was probably due to the (at least numerical) dominance of scholars from Germany among the participants in these events that the deconstructive approach remained comparatively marginal. Above all, however, the choice of the topic "materialities of communication" for the fourth colloquium marked yet another yearning for a "harder" intellectual style and, in this specific case, for a range of "harder" topics.

It should have become evident by now that I understand the alternation between "soft" and "hard" practices within the humanities as a late reaction to their birth trauma as a cluster of academic disciplines whose main point of convergence and identity was an exclusion, namely, the exclusion of the epistemological dimensions of perception and reference.[28] But this thesis is not yet an answer to the question with which the present chapter began: Why we are so eager to "overcome metaphysics." One answer made possible by this chapter is that "overcoming metaphysics" can be seen, in retrospect, as an attempt to redeem ourselves from that ultimately pointless alternation between "soft" and "hard" intellectual practices. I hope therefore that my interest in the emergence of meaning and, above all, in the oscillation between meaning effects and presence effects, so different from the topic of "materialities of communication," will no longer be attributed exclusively to one or the other of these two polarities (between which literary studies—and, tendentially, the humanities at large—have been caught for many decades now). If it is not *the* solution of how to "overcome metaphysics" or of "how to leave metaphysics behind," breaking with the alternation between soft and hard paradigms could at least be a way of escaping (or of forgetting) metaphysics as an intellectual force field. The other—more important but less "epistemological"—answer to the question of why we want to "overcome metaphysics" so badly is that we feel, intuitively at least, that the metaphysical worldview is related to what I have called a "loss of world." This is one important reason for our feeling that we are no longer in touch with the things of the world.

Beyond Meaning: Positions and Concepts in Motion

1

One of my very favorite quotations has long been a passage from the first chapter of Jacques Derrida's *Of Grammatology* in which the author writes about the "age of the sign" (and I think he refers to what I have been calling "metaphysics") in a perhaps deliberately mild paradoxical tone (but in a paradoxical tone nevertheless). More precisely, we read that the "age of the sign" will "perhaps never *end*. Its historical *closure*, however, is outlined."[1] This has been and still is, by any means, a both compact and clear description of deconstruction's position on the issue of the (impossible or possible) end of metaphysics—and it probably even continues to be a good description of what one may want to characterize, from outside deconstruction, as a more or less institutionalized intellectual position within the humanities at large. There are good arguments for bringing the age of the polarity between the purely material signifier and the purely spiritual signified to closure, but it is not obvious—certainly not from Derrida's text—that we really want to use these arguments in a way that would definitely mean the end of metaphysics. At least from my point of view, then, the most urgent question is: Who will be patient enough—infinitely patient enough—to agree with Derrida? For, after all, not ending what has been brought to a potential closure must look like a position of willfully accepted suffering, a position that also, not by coincidence, of course, resembles the basic structure of Paul de Man's continually reiterated mourning over the incapacity of human language to signify or to refer to the things of the world. De Man was claiming that he had brought the illusion of what he called "semiotic reading" to closure—but by so faithfully mourning the loss of reference and of stable meaning, he made it impossible ever to leave them behind.

Now what would it mean—and what would it take—to put an end to the age of the sign? What would it mean—and what would it take—to end metaphysics? It can certainly not mean that we would abandon meaning, signification, and interpretation. Linking up with the previous chapter, I think that the "beyond" in metaphysics can only mean doing something in addition to interpretation—without, of course, abandoning interpretation as an elementary and probably inevitable intellectual practice. It would mean to try and develop concepts that could allow us, in the Humanities, to relate to the world in a way that is more complex than interpretation alone, that is more complex than only attributing meaning to the world (or, to use an older topology, that is more complex than extracting meaning from the world). The effort that it would take us to develop noninterpretative in addition to hermeneutic concepts would therefore be an effort directed against the consequences and taboos coming from the enthronement of interpretation as the *exclusive* core practice of the humanities. The difficulty of such an effort to develop a repertoire of noninterpretative concepts for the humanities would (or will) lie in the simple fact that, as a result of the dominance of the Cartesian world picture since early modernity and of hermeneutics since the early twentieth century, it seems literally impossible in our intellectual world, at least at first glance, to come up with concepts that may satisfy the goal of practicing (and grounding) something that is not interpretation.

Derrida has never been shy about inventing new concepts, even when the need to do so has not been very obvious. Why is he so hesitant, then, about coming up with some new concept that would allow us to "end" the age of the sign? I think he has refrained from such an attempt because he anticipates (perhaps correctly) that this would make "getting his hands dirty" unavoidable (although doing so "as a humanist" is not very dirty to start with). What I want to say in this rather colloquial fashion is that there is probably no way to end the exclusive dominance of interpretation, to abandon hermeneutics and metaphysics in the humanities without using concepts that potential intellectual opponents may polemically characterize as "substantialist," that is, concepts such as "substance" itself, "presence," and perhaps even "reality" and "Being." To use such concepts, however, has long been a symptom of despicably bad intellectual taste in the humanities; indeed, to believe in the possibility of referring to the world other than by meaning has become synonymous with the utmost degree of philosophical naïveté —and, until very recently, few humanists have been courageous enough to deliberately draw such potentially devastating and embarrassing criticism upon themselves. We all know only too well that saying whatever it takes to confute the charge of being "substantialist" is the humanities on autopilot. For many years now, the smashing success of deconstruction has depended on every deconstructor's willingness to hurl the charge of naïveté, or at least of being "substantialist," at whoever tries to argue in favor of a not exclusively meaning-based relationship to the world—and even

at those who, much more modestly, try to argue in favor of the
possibility of identifying and maintaining some stable meaning.
Despite all its revolutionary claims, and its confidence that it has
the intellectual potential to bring "the age of the sign" to "closure," deconstruction has thus to a large extent relied on soft ter-
ror to shore up the existing order in the humanities.[2]

2

From the point of view of these academic taboos, I get my hands
awfully dirty in this chapter, for I try in it to reach and to think a
layer in cultural objects and in our relation to them that is not
the layer of meaning. While I hasten to emphasize the obvious,
namely, that this will by no means be a life-threatening move, it
might be good to point to a number of important affinities
within the contemporary scene of the humanities—if I want at
least some colleagues and their students to read me, and if I want
to avoid the potential impression that the only driving force behind my argument may be a (very!) belatedly adolescent revolt
against the highest authorities of the professional world that I
inhabit (or an even more belated—indeed, infantile—pleasure in
getting my hands dirty). For the purpose of underlining my own
position on the contemporary map of the humanities, however,
it might be a convenient idea to start my list of affinities on the
opposite side, that is, with a philosopher with whom I share
many readings and questions—but whose recent work, quite hy-
perbolically and even programmatically, goes in the opposite direction.

I am referring to Gianni Vattimo and, more specifically, to his
book *Beyond Interpretation*.[3] Vattimo belongs to those maximalists within present-day hermeneutics who are convinced that the
belief (for him, of course, more than "belief") that interpretation

is our only possible way of referring to the world has long
reached the sciences and has consequently diluted all scientific
facticity claims: "The world as a conflict of interpretations and
nothing more is not an image of the world that has to be de-
fended against the realism and positivism of science. It is modern
science, heir and completion of metaphysics, that turns the world
into a place where there are no (longer) facts, only interpretations."⁴ Of all hermeneutic maximalists, of all humanists who
hold interpretation to be humankind's exclusive way of relating
to the world, I choose to quote Vattimo here because his book
also shows, in civilized and yet sufficiently aggressive terms, that
gestures of intellectual intimidation against those who might be
tempted to use any "substantialist" concepts have indeed become
a strategy that powerfully supports hermeneutic maximalism. In
this spirit, Vattimo proposes a maximally hermeneutic reaction
"against the grain" to Heidegger's conception of a "history of
Being" (*Seinsgeschichte*)—a conception to which I shall return
later in this chapter, reading it myself as an encouragement for
breaking the taboo established by the humanities against all potentially "nonhermeneutic," that is, "substantialist," language.
Now Vattimo and I would probably agree on what Heidegger
meant by "history of Being"—but our reactions to this concept
are as different as can be. While I want to turn the substantiality
of Being against the universality claim of endless interpretation,
Vattimo wants Being (the desire for Being?) to disappear under
an endless reiteration of interpretations: "the reading that I propose of the history of Being [is its reading] as the story of a 'long
goodbye', of an interminable weakening of Being. In this case,
the overcoming of Being is understood only as a recollection of
the oblivion of Being, never as making Being present again, not
even as a term that always lies beyond every formulation."⁵ That

Vattimo, in addition, calls his antipresence, antisubstantialist position a "leftist reading of Heidegger" shows what I mean when I am saying that hermeneutics and interpretation, within the humanists' discourse, are protected by gestures of intellectual intimidation. For who in the humanities could afford to be accused, simultaneously, of being "substantialist" and, in addition, of "not-being-of-the-Left"?

Umberto Eco might be the one colleague to survive such a daring double provocation. He has indeed made the untimely claim of returning to a form of textual interpretation that, instead of being an endless production of variants, might produce definitive results or might at least yield criteria that allow one to distinguish between better or worse interpretations. "The limits of interpretation," says Eco when trying to explain the title of a collection of his essays, "coincide with the rights of the text (which does not mean with the rights of the author)."[6] But while Eco must hope to ground such traditional interpretation *rediviva* in some kind of world-reference, at least in a reference to the text as an object without ambiguities, and while he is thus already leaving the confines that phenomenology and the humanities had subsequently set for themselves within the hermeneutic field and/as the classical subject/object paradigm, there is reason to doubt that, after all the crises in the history of twentieth-century Western philosophy, such a willful return to epistemological naïveté can ultimately be viable. For it is the subject/object paradigm that today excludes any easy world-reference—and it is this very paradigm that Eco leaves untouched (or inadvertently restores) when he commits to "the rights of the text." This precisely is why I believe that we should try to reestablish our contact with the things of the world outside the subject/object paradigm (or in a modified version of it) and by avoiding interpretation—without even criticizing the highly sophisticated and highly self-reflexive art of interpretation that the humanities have long established.

This also is why I feel such a strong affinity with the point of departure of Jean-Luc Nancy's book *The Birth to Presence*—where I even find a (for me at least) very familiar feeling of frustration with the kind of position in contemporary philosophy that Vattimo represents: "A moment arrives when one can no longer feel anything but anger, an absolute anger, against so many discourses, so many texts that have no other care than to make a little more sense, to redo or to perfect delicate works of signification."[7] The presence for which Nancy is longing, as an alternative to all those discourses that produce just "a little more sense," is certainly not the self-reflexive presence that Derrida had criticized in Husserl's philosophy. Nancy, on the contrary, is alluding to a conception of presence that is difficult—if not impossible—to reconcile with modern Western epistemology, because it brings back the dimension of physical closeness and tangibility: "'The delight of presence' is the mystical formula par excellence," and such presence that escapes the dimension of meaning has to be in tension with the principle of representation: "Presence does not come without effacing the presence that representation would like to designate (its fundament, its origin, its subject)."[8] At the same time, among the authors to whom I want to refer in order to mark contemporary affinities with my own point of departure, Nancy is also the first who points to the certainty (an almost "practical" certainty, based primarily on experience, rather than a certainty based on conceptual deduction) that, under today's conditions at least, and different in this sense from the conception of "real presence" in medieval theology, presence cannot become part of a permanent situation, it can never be something that, so to speak, we would be able to hold on to.

This must be the reason why Nancy (and, with him, quite a number of philosophers interested in phenomena of presence) associate this concept with what I call conditions of "extreme temporality." Presence, for Nancy, at least presence under contemporary conditions, is birth, "the coming that effaces itself and brings itself back." No other thinker, probably, has developed the very motif of "extreme temporality" with richer conceptual results than Karl Heinz Bohrer. Unlike Nancy, however, Bohrer hardly ever focuses on the concept of presence itself. For him, "suddenness," the ephemeral character of certain appearances and departures, is the central feature of aesthetic experience, and he refers to it as "aesthetic negativity": "the negativity of the awareness of vanishing presence."[9] That which becomes apparent, under such conditions, in Bohrer's concept of aesthetic experience, is obviously substance, not meaning. But it seems to be, exclusively, the substance of the signifier. Referring, for example, to Kafka's famous reflection about the impression that a group of Jewish actors made on him, Bohrer writes: "Kafka does not read the expression of the actor in relation to what the actor expresses (i.e., his role), he only reads from the expression."[10]

After Nancy's and Bohrer's insistence on "extreme temporality," what interests me in George Steiner's reflection on "real presences" is the attention that he dedicates to the relationship (or should we rather say to the mutual interpenetration?) of layers of meaning and layers of substantive presence in a work of art.[11] Steiner wants the effect of presence to come from a "wager" on divine presence in the full theological sense of these words:

> [the] wager—it is that of Descartes, of Kant and of every poet, artist, composer of whom we have explicit record—predicates the

presence of a realness, of a "substantiation" (the theological reach of this word is obvious) within language and form. It supposes a passage, beyond the fictive or the purely pragmatic, from meaning to meaningfulness. The conjecture is that "God" *is*, not because our grammar is outworn; but that grammar lives and generates words because there is the wager on God. Such a conjecture may, wherever it has been or is put forward, be wholly erroneous.[12]

Let us leave aside the question of whether speaking about that desire for presence must entail, willingly or not, a participation in this theological wager.[13] For once he has laid open his own theological implication, Steiner tends to fill the place of substantial presence with the material features of different types of works of art:

The arts are most wonderfully rooted in substance, in the human body, in stone, in pigment, in the twanging of gut or the weight of wind on reeds. All good art and literature begin in immanence. But they do not stop there. Which is to say, very plainly, that it is the enterprise and privilege of the aesthetic to quicken into presence the continuum between temporality and eternity, between matter and spirit, between man and 'the other.'[14]

In a different context, Steiner writes about the coming into being of "energized and signifying form from within."[15] The form of the work of art is "energized" (this is how I understand Steiner) because its presence has been "externalized, actualized"—in a movement probably triggered by the specific situational context in which the work of art can unfold its powers (I shall return to some questions regarding this specific context in the following chapter).[16] But at the same time, the form of the work of art continues to be a signifying form, producing a tension with form as being "energized."

A third aspect that I find important and enriching in the work

of some contemporary authors who, like myself, are fascinated by
the philosophical issues of presence, is their critique of a school
of thought that, with a certain degree of pride, has come to call
itself "constructivism" in recent decades. An admittedly mali-
cious way of characterizing constructivism would be to say that it
is a rundown version of phenomenology's point of departure according to which only the contents of human consciousness can
be the object of philosophical analysis. Based on a necessary consequence of this position, that is, on the postulate that whatever
we identify as "reality/realities" can then only be dealt with as a
projection or as a "construction" of our consciousness, supple-
mented by the more precarious double claim that it is possible to
identify, in these constructions, features of a consciousness
shared by all humans (the "transcendental subject"), and that we
can find traces of those shared features in all existing societies
("lifeworlds"), constructivism finally leads to the conclusion that
all realities that we share with other humans are "social constructions." Counter, I think, to its philosophical origins, constructivism has turned today into the banal belief that everything
from "sex" via "culture" to "landscape" is at the easy disposition
of the human will to change—because everything is "but a human construction." It was Judith Butler's *Bodies That Matter*
(1993), her most important book so far, that first provoked constructivism as a widely accepted basis of the ongoing discussions
in gender philosophy by bringing back into the debate the "materiality" of the body and the inertia that this materiality of the
body offers to any kind of transformation: "What I would propose in place of these conceptions of construction is a return to
the notion of matter, not as a site or surface, but as a process of
materialization that stabilizes over time to produce the effect of
boundary, fixity, and surface we call matter."[17] What Butler

means is that a simple decision is by no means enough to change one's gender, as constructivism seems to suggest; what it requires are forms of behavior and action maintained over time (Butler uses the concept of "performance" in this context) that are capable of shaping and producing different body forms and body identities. But while Butler is quite explicit in her critique of constructivism, it also becomes clear that she is well aware of the discursive taboo that protects its position. This, of course, is the taboo that disqualifies the use of all concepts related to "substance" or "reality" as intellectual poor taste. And even Judith Butler feels compelled to yield to the threat of being accused of such bad taste by confessing that she feels a certain degree of "anxiety"—so much so that she ends up presenting herself in the mildly paradoxical role of a constructivist who believes in substantial bodily differences:

> The critic might also suspect the constructivist of a certain somato-phobia and seek assurances that this abstracted theorist will admit that there are, minimally, sexually differentiated parts, activities, capacities, hormonal and chromosomal differences that can be conceded without reference to "construction." Although at this moment I want to offer an absolute reassurance to my interlocutor, some anxiety prevails. To "concede" the undeniability of "sex" or its "materiality" is always to concede some version of "sex," some formation of "materiality."[18]

Concentrating on the question of how bodily substance can be transformed—a question that, to my knowledge, has never been excluded by any philosophy working with the concept of "substance"—Butler wants to show that it is possible to abandon the constructivist doxa without giving up the political value of the subject's right and ability to change.

In a similarly groundbreaking book, which analyzes the hu-

man mimetic faculty as a faculty of embodied imitation, the an-
thropologist Michael Taussig finds himself caught in a polemic
with constructivism similar to Judith Butler's. Thanks to a less
politically charged intellectual environment, however, Taussig is
far more confident than Butler in the critical and often even
ironic parts of his argument:

> When it was enthusiastically pointed out within memory of our
> present Academy that race or gender or nation . . . were so many
> social constructions, inventions, and representations, a window was
> opened, an invitation to begin the critical prospect of analysis and
> cultural reconstruction was offered. . . . The brilliance of the pro-
> nouncement was blinding. Nobody was asking what's the next
> step? What do we do with this old insight? If life is constructed,
> how come it appears so immutable? How come culture appears so
> natural?[19]

Taussig not only points, once again, to what he calls, with a deliberate pleonasm, "the true real" of substance and materiality (as
that which makes culture appear "so natural" and as the "next
step" of analysis beyond constructivism); he also begins to his-
toricize the desire for a different epistemology by postulating a
relationship between new technical arrays and a "recharging" of
the mimetic faculty that relies on embodiment:

> [I]f I am correct in involving a certain magic of the signifier and
> what Walter Benjamin took the mimetic faculty to be—namely,
> the compulsion to become the Other—and if, thanks to new social
> conditions and new techniques of reproduction (such as cinema
> and mass production of imagery), modernity has ushered in a veri-
> table rebirth, a recharging and retooling the mimetic faculty, then
> it seems to me that we are forthwith invited if not forced into the
> inner sanctum of mimetic mysteries where, in imitating, we will
> find distance from the imitated and hence gain some release from

the suffocating hold of "constructivism" and the dreadful passive
view of nature it upholds.[20]

Even closer to my own concerns, at least closer to the concerns
of my academic discipline (and as close to this book as Taussig's
work, in terms of the epistemological premises), is the German
philosopher Martin Seel's proposal to ground a new reflection on
aesthetics in the concept of "appearance."[21] Under "appearance"
Seel subsumes the conditions through which the world is given
to us and presents itself to the human senses (another word that
he uses in the same context is *Wahrnehmung:* "perception"). Obviously, an aesthetics of appearance tries to bring back to our
consciousness and to our bodies the thingness of the world. Appearance is also in tension, inevitably, with the dominant interpretative approach that permeates our everyday relationship to
the world up to the point of making us forget that it necessarily
implies a layer different from meaning. Not randomly, therefore,
Seel repeatedly associates appearance with presence—and whatever "appears" is "present" because it makes itself available to the
human senses. There are two aspects to which he gives particular
emphasis. In the first place, the appearance of things, for Seel,
always produces an awareness of the limitations of human control over these things (*Unverfügbarkeit*). Secondly, and this
seems to be the central question of Seel's reflection, he tries to
identify and to understand those conditions and devices through
which appearance can be produced in a social and cultural environment where meaning attribution—and not sensual perception—is institutionally primordial in the ways in which we deal
with the world.

But I have kept the most surprising—and perhaps also the
most persuasive—affinity for the end of this part of my argument. In an interview that he gave toward the end of his life,

Hans-Georg Gadamer who, more than any other philosopher of
our times, had become associated with hermeneutics (including
its universality claim) and with interpretation as an ongoing
production of meaning, suggested a greater acknowledgment of
the nonsemantic, that is, material components of literary texts.
When cautiously asked by his interlocutor whether it might be
the function of these nonsemantic features in a poem, for example, to challenge the "hermeneutic identity" of the text, Gadamer
replied by developing a much more radical position, a position
that, indeed, undercuts the assumption that meaning is always
and necessarily the dominant dimension in the reading of a
poem:

> But—can we really assume that the reading of such texts is a read-
> ing exclusively concentrated on meaning? Do we not sing these
> texts [*Ist es nicht ein Singen*]? Should the process in which a poem
> speaks only be carried by a meaning intention? Is there not, at the
> same time, a truth that lies in its performance [*eine Vollzugswahr-
> heit*]? This, I think, is the task with which the poem confronts us.[22]

Gadamer calls the nonhermeneutic dimension of the literary text
its "volume" (*Volumen*), and he equates the tension between its
semantic and its nonsemantic components with the tension between "world" and "earth" that Heidegger develops in his essay
"The Origin of the Work of Art." It is the component of "earth"
that enables the work of art, or the poem, to "stand in itself"; it is
"earth" that gives the work of art existence in space.[23]

3

From a perspective of intellectual genealogy, Gadamer's reference
to Heidegger is not surprising at all, because he belonged to the
first generation of Heidegger's students. But the connection that

Gadamer draws between the nonhermeneutic dimension in the reading of a poem and Heidegger's essay "The Origin of the Work of Art" has a much broader significance in my argument. For all the authors whose works I have been discussing so far as part of an intellectual environment that wants to go "beyond meaning attribution" (which is also beyond hermeneutics's claim to universality) remain quite hesitant as soon as they touch upon the challenge of designing the alternative repertoire of concepts that such a move "beyond meaning" would make necessary. In the previous chapter, I said in passing that the Aristotelian tradition could be—at least—a source of inspiration for the development of such a repertoire; in this chapter, I shall use medieval culture (a culture that was so thoroughly Aristotelian that the name "Aristotle" became synonymous with the noun "philosopher") for this very same purpose.

But the one philosopher from our not so remote intellectual past who quite programmatically—and over several decades—produced such a repertoire of nonmetaphysical concepts is, of course, Martin Heidegger. Although many of Heidegger's present-day interpreters like to bracket this aspect of his self-understanding, Heidegger himself wanted *Being and Time,* the book in which the full scope of his thought became visible for the first time, to be an "*ontology* in the broadest sense of the word and without any affinities to existing ontological directions and tendencies."[24] As an ontology, however, his philosophy inscribed itself into the intellectual movement of the "conservative revolution" that, above all during the 1920s, embodied and articulated a widespread discontent with the intellectual loss of the world outside human consciousness that the philosophy of Heidegger's mentor Edmund Husserl had come to represent.[25] From Heidegger's perspective at least, Husserl's phenomenology was merely

the endpoint of a millenary philosophical trajectory in which the
subject/object paradigm—that is, the conceptual configuration
of the ongoing divergence between human existence and the
world, based on the contrast between human existence as purely
spiritual and the world as a purely material sphere—had led
Western culture to an extreme state of alienation from the world.
More than Husserl (who, with good reason, liked to call his
philosophy "Cartesian"), Descartes was the explicit object of
Heidegger's critique: this is why *Being and Time* presents the
Cartesian grounding of human existence on thought (and on
thought alone) and the subsequent dissociations between human
existence and space and between human existence and substance
as the original sins of modern philosophy.[26] Seen from this perspective, the decisive conceptual move in Heidegger's book is, as
I have already mentioned, the characterization of human existence as "being-in-the-world," that is, as an existence that is always already in a substantial and therefore in a spatial contact
with the things of the world.[27]

"Being-in-the-world" is a perfectly suitable concept for a type
of reflection and analysis that tries to recuperate the presence
components in our relationship to the things of the world. On
the following pages, however, I would like to unfold the complexity of another Heideggerean key concept, a concept that was
hardly developed yet in *Being and Time,* but that I think is
closely related to the aspect of substantiality. This is the concept
of "Being"—and I have two reasons for emphasizing it. Firstly,
"Being" is the notion in Heidegger's philosophy that has posed
the most problems for all the different attempts at integrating his
thought into more conventional systems. Being has also been the
one concept that can never avoid falling under the anathema of
"intellectual poor taste" in contemporary mainstream thinking

(above all, in "constructivism"). Secondly, I hope that the effort to unfold several dimensions of Heidegger's concept of "Being" will produce a clearer awareness of how profound a transformation our current conceptual style would have to undergo if we seriously tried to develop a discourse that was more suitable for the intellectual (and perhaps not exclusively intellectual) fascination with presence. At any event, it is much less the idea (or the utopia) of a full appropriation of Heidegger's concept of "Being" for such a project that has motivated my concentration here than the hope that a confrontation with this concept of "Being" might broaden our minds (to use an embarrassingly "pedagogical" expression) and thus help us to think beyond the limits of the metaphysical tradition.

In what follows, then, I shall try to establish four different perspectives that at least begin to give an account of the complexity and of the thought-provoking eccentricity of this notion ("eccentricity" within the metaphysical tradition that has so thoroughly permeated our thought).[28] My first thesis is that "Being," within the architecture of Heidegger's philosophy, takes over the place of truth (or, more precisely: the place of the content of truth), which had been occupied, since the times of Plato and of early Platonism, by the "ideas" (or by other forms of conceptual configurations), and that Being is *not* something conceptual. Heidegger is indeed concerned with redefining truth—but Being does not simply substitute truth. Rather, Heidegger talks about truth as something that happens (*ein Geschehen*).[29] In principle, this happening is a double movement of unconcealing and hiding—whose structure I shall try to describe in more detail as we go along in this reflection on the concept of Being. Being is that which is both unconcealed and hidden in the happening of truth. Due to this position in the happening of

truth, Heidegger leaves no doubt, Being, as it is being unconcealed, for example, in a work of art, is not something spiritual
or something conceptual. Being is not a meaning. Being belongs
to the dimension of things. This is why Heidegger can say about
the happening of truth in works of art: "Art works universally
display a thingly character, albeit in a wholly distinct way."[30]
Saying that it is the function of a work of art to "show something
that has the character of a thing," the German original text states
this point in a much less ambiguous fashion.[31] If Being has the
character of a thing, this means that it has substance and that,
therefore (and unlike anything purely spiritual), it occupies
space. This explains why Heidegger writes in his *Introduction to
Metaphysics* of "entering a landscape"—and I don't think that
the reference is metaphorical—when he tries to describe what it
means to have recuperated, in his philosophy, the long-lost
question of Being: "Through our questioning, we are entering a
landscape; to be in this landscape is the fundamental prerequisite
for restoring the rootedness to historical Dasein."[32] Having a
substance and thus occupying space also implies the possibility
of Being unfolding a movement: "Being as *phusis* is the merging
sway."[33]

My second thesis is that Being's movement in space turns out
to be multidimensional (tridimensional, to be precise) and that,
in its full complexity, this multidimensional movement accounts
for what Heidegger calls the "happening of truth." The following passage from Heidegger's *Introduction to Metaphysics* refers to
the first two (out of three) directions in the movement of Being,
which, extrapolating from Heidegger's own words, I would like
to label "vertical" ("sway") and "horizontal ("idea," "look"):

Phusis is the emerging sway, the standing-there-on-itself, constancy.
Idea, the look as what is seen, is a determination of the constant as,

and only insofar as, it stands opposite to seeing. But *phusis* as emerging sway is also already appearing. To be sure, it is just that appearing has two meanings. First, appearing denotes the self-gathering event of bringing-itself-to-stand and thus standing in gatheredness. But then, appearing also means: as something that is already standing there, to proffer a foreground, a surface, a look as an offering to be looked at.[34]

I think it is appropriate to associate the vertical dimension in the movement of Being with its simple being there (or, more precisely, with its emergence into being there and with occupying a space), whereas the horizontal dimension points to Being as being perceived, which also means to Being offering itself to somebody's view (as an appearance and as an "ob-ject," as something that moves "toward" or "against" an observer). The third dimension in the movement of Being is a dimension of withdrawal. In "Zur Erörterung der Gelassenheit," written in 1944/45, Heidegger suggests that Being "rather withdraws itself instead of offering itself to us," so that "the things that appear" in the clearing of Being, "no longer have the character of objects."[35] I am convinced that this withdrawal is part of the double movement of "unconcealment" and "withdrawal" that, as we have already seen, constitutes the happening of truth, and that the part of "unconcealment" contains both the vertical movement of "sway" (of emergence and its result: being there) and the horizontal movement of "idea" (as presenting itself, appearance).

But why would the happening of truth consist of a double movement whose vectors go in opposite directions?[36] Any attempt at solving this problem makes it necessary for us to venture a further assumption about what Being might be—beyond its having a substance, an articulation in space, and a triple movement. My further assumption about the concept of "Being"

is, then, that it is meant to refer to the things of the world independently of (or prior to) their interpretation and their structuring through any network of historically or culturally specific
concepts. In other words, Being, I think, refers to the things of
the world before they become part of a culture (or, using the
rhetorical figure of the paradox, the concept refers to the things
of the world before they become part of a world).[37] If we exclude
the idea that Being might just be that which has no structure,
the double movement of unconcealment and withdrawal could
then be explained in the following way: Being will only be Being
outside the networks of semantics and other cultural distinctions.
For us to experience Being, however, it would, on the one hand,
have to cross the threshold between a sphere (which we can at
least imagine) free from the grids of any specific culture and, on
the other hand, the well-structured spheres of different cultures.
Again, in order to be experienced, Being would have to become
part of a culture. As soon, however, as Being crosses this threshold, it is, of course, no longer Being. This is why the unconcealment of Being, in the happening of truth, has to realize itself as
an ongoing double movement of coming forth (toward the
threshold) and of withdrawing (away from the threshold), of unconcealment and of hiding. Heidegger seems to see this double
movement playing out on at least two different levels. Certainly,
the tension between coming forth and withdrawal is a configuration that we all know, so to speak, from our personal experience of acts of world-experience. But the same structure is also
constitutive of Heidegger's much larger conception of a "History
of Being" (*Seinsgeschichte*). Whether Being unconceals itself or
not does not only depend on the (greater or lesser) composure
that each *Dasein* is capable of investing. It also depends on each
specific moment in the time of humankind. In this sense, Hei-

degger was convinced, for example, that ancient Greece had an incomparably better chance of being present in the unconcealment of Being than, say, inhabitants of the early twentieth century. Seen from this angle, from the angle of a withdrawal that can never be entirely overcome, Being is not "benign"—or at least never as benign as that which is given to humankind in the Christian concept of revelation.[38]

My third thesis is about the role of *Dasein* (Heidegger's word for "human existence") in the happening of truth. In order to understand this aspect, it is important to keep in mind that *Dasein* is not synonymous with the standard definitions of "subject" or "subjectivity," which is to say, it is different from the concept of "subjectivity" that belongs to the epistemological context of the subject/object paradigm. *Dasein* is being-in-the-world, that is, human existence that is always already in—both spatial and functional—contact with the world. This world with which *Dasein* is in touch is "ready-to-hand," it is an always already interpreted world. Presupposing the situation of being-in-the-world, Heidegger characterizes *Dasein*'s possible contribution to the unconcealment of Being as composure (*Gelassenheit*), the capacity of letting things be. The impulse or initiative for the unconcealment of Being (if such words can be adequate at all) therefore seems to come from the side of Being, not from the side of *Dasein*. Interestingly, then, a further determination of composure is its status of being "outside the distinction between activity and passivity."[39] Inasmuch as *Dasein*, for Heidegger, has to be in-the-world (and cannot be in-front-of-the-world, like a subject),[40] it is also plausible that he describes composure as the capacity to "abandon any transcending imagination and projection."[41] Clearly, *Dasein* is not supposed to occupy a position that can be associated with manipulating, transforming, or interpreting the world.

Finally, I want to discuss Heidegger's tendency, manifest in many different books and texts throughout his work, to present the work of art as a privileged site for the happening of truth, that is, for the unconcealment (and the withdrawal) of Being. In this context, I must stress that, despite attacks of insecurity that sometimes come over me, as a literary critic venturing into the field of philosophy, I do not, of course, draw any jubilant or triumphant feelings from the privileged epistemological status that Heidegger gives to the work of art[42] (or from the trend among contemporary Western philosophers of reevaluating the importance of aesthetics from a similar perspective). My main interest in Heidegger's analysis of the work of art is simply based on the place that he gives, in this context, to the concept of Being. Here is a passage from "The Origin of the Work of Art" that brings to a point of convergence some of the aspects that I have been putting together thus far—the happening of truth as making us see things in a way "different from the ordinary way," for example, and this "different" way being associated with "nothing," that is, with a dimension where all cultural distinctions are absent:

> *Art then is the becoming and happening of truth.* Does truth, then, arise out of nothing? It does indeed if by nothing is meant the mere not of that which is, and if we here think of that which is as an object present in the ordinary way, which thereafter comes to light and is challenged by the existence of the work as only presumptively a true being. Truth is never gathered from objects that are present and ordinary. Rather, the opening up of the Open, and the clearing of what is, happens only as the openness is projected.[43]

Now, where might Heidegger's specific association between the work of art and the unconcealment of Being come from? The least we can say is that, in its basic outline, the back-and-forth movement that he sees in the unconcealment of Being is a structure that, on different levels and in different contexts, he also frequently points to when he thematizes the work of art. There is certainly no reason to believe that Heidegger wanted to describe the work of art as the only site where the unconcealment of Being was possible. On the other hand, his texts suggest that he saw the work of art as a medium where the happening of truth was more of a possibility (or should I say more of a probability?) than elsewhere.

But "The Origin of the Work of Art" also provides further answers to what the word "Being" might possibly mean (as opposed to the question of how the unconcealment of Being can happen). In the middle of the text, Heidegger dwells, for several pages, on his recollection of an ancient Greek temple, and it is there that he develops two further concepts, "world" and "earth," in his attempt to characterize Being. Of course, the relationship between the temple as a work of art and unconcealed Being is not one of representation: "A building, a Greek temple, portrays nothing."[44] A complex answer to the question of how the presence of the temple can contribute to making the unconcealment of Being happen is offered in the contrasting descriptions of "world" and "earth": "The world is the self-disclosing openness of the broad paths of the simple and essential decisions in the destiny of a historical people. The earth is the spontaneous forthcoming of that which is continually self-secluding and to that extent sheltering and concealing."[45] What exactly is the difference between the roles that "earth" and "world" are supposed to play in the happening of truth? Regarding the aspect of "earth," the elements that we have accumulated thus far for the understanding of the concept of "Being," on the one hand, and Heidegger's evocation of the temple, on the other, converge in the impression that the sheer presence of the temple triggers the unconcealment

of a number of things—in their thingness—that surround the
temple:

> Standing there, the building rests on the rocky ground. This resting
> of the work draws up out of the rock the mystery of that rock's
> clumsy yet spontaneous support. Standing there, the building holds
> its ground against the storm raging above it and so first makes the
> storm itself manifest in its violence. The luster and gleam of the
> stone, though itself apparently glowing only by the grace of the sun,
> yet first brings to light the light of the day, the breadth of the sky,
> the darkness of the night.[46]

The central idea in these sentences about "earth" is deceptively
easy. Only the presence of certain things (in this case, the presence of the temple) opens up the possibility of other things appearing in their primordial material qualities—and this effect
might be considered as one way (and as a part) of unconcealing
their Being.

It is much more complicated to figure out in which way the
concept "world" can help us grasp the concept of Being. For if
unconcealed Being has the character of a thing (thus our first
thesis), of a thing independent of its integration into any semantic network, this seems to be incompatible with "world" being
something as culturally specific (it appears) as "the simple and
essential decisions in the destiny of a historical people"—with
which words Heidegger tries to illustrate the example of a world
given by a God's presence in the Greek temple. And he continues:

> By means of the temple, the god is present in the temple. This
> presence of the god is in itself the extension and delimitation of the
> precinct as a holy precinct. The temple and its precinct, however,
> do not fade into the indefinite. It is the temple-work that first fits
> together and at the same time gathers around itself the unity of

those paths and relations in which birth and death, disaster and blessing, victory and disgrace, endurance and decline acquire the shape of destiny for human being.[47]

Clearly, "world" is meant to have a spatial articulation, and it is described as an integrative dimension, as a dimension that brings things together. Based on this premise, I see two solutions to the problem of how "world," "earth," and "Being" could be related. One possibility is to try and understand Heidegger's references to concepts like "destiny" or to the Greek "god" as references to integrative dimensions that are less culturally and historically specific than we might have imagined at first glance. It is thus not impossible to think, of different "destinies" or of different "gods," that they belong to the side of Being (it is indeed quite conventional, at least from a theological point of view, to think of "gods" as withdrawn from any historically specific everyday worlds). If we further try to imagine "destinies" and "gods" as overarching, as integrative modalities within Being, rather than individual "things" within Being, then such modalities could shape things in a way that would not depend on historically spe-cific cultures. This would mean, for example, and always on the side of Being, that earth, and sea, and sky are different each time, in the presence of or belonging to different gods or to different destinies. Such a speculation brings out one very important and often overlooked aspect in Heidegger's text. This is the idea that seeing things as part of Being, that is, independently of the shapes imposed upon them by historically specific cultures, does not mean that these things have either no forms at all or neces-sarily unchanging ("eternal") forms. We should then not assume that, for example, Being unconcealed to an ancient Greek peas-ant or philosopher would have been the same as Being that could be unconcealed to us, two and a half millennia later. "Earth" could refer to Being as substance and "world" to the changing configurations and structures of which Being as substance can become a part. But these changes of "world" would have nothing to do with the dimension to which we normally refer as "historical" or "cultural" change.

The other solution regarding the status of "world" is somewhat easier to grasp, and it leads to the exclusion of "world" from the dimension of Being.[48] It interprets Heidegger to mean that Being always and only unconceals itself in the form and in the substance (as well as against or through the form and the substance) of things that are part of specific cultures ("beings" and "worlds" as configurations of such things). For, unlike the Platonic ideas, Being is not supposed to be something general or something metahistorical "below" or "behind" a world of surfaces. Perhaps it is as simple as this proposal for a definition: Being is tangible things, seen independently of their culturally specific situations—which is neither an easy feat to achieve nor a probable thing to happen. Heidegger senses a tension, even a struggle in the relationship between "world" (configurations of things in the context of specific cultural situations?) and "earth" (things seen independently of their specific cultural situations?). "Earth" or Being (*Sein*) and "world" or "beings" (*das Seiende*), according to this reading, belong inseparably together—but in order "to self-assert their natures," they have to diverge within this togetherness: "The opposition of world and earth is a striving. But we would surely all too easily falsify its nature if we were to confound striving with discord and dispute, and thus see it only as disorder and destruction. In essential striving, rather, the opponents raise each other into the self-assertion of their natures."[49]

One thing seems to be certain, independently of our interpretations of the concept "world." Whenever a specific cultural situation vanishes ("if the god flees from the temple"), then the things belonging to that situation can no longer be the starting point for an unconcealment of Being, because they lack "world" as the integrative dimension, which seems to give them vitality: "The temple, in its standing there, first gives to things their look and to men their outlook on themselves. This view remains open as long as the work is a work, as long as the god has not fled from it."[50]

However provisional my attempt at unfolding the complexities of Heidegger's concept of "Being" may remain, there cannot be any doubt that this concept is very close to the concept of "presence" (which I have tried to identify, at the beginning of this chapter, as the point of convergence between different contemporary reflections that try to go beyond a metaphysical epistemology and an exclusively meaning-based relationship to the world). Both concepts, Being and presence, imply substance; both are related to space; both can be associated with movement. Heidegger may not have elaborated the dimension of "extreme temporality" as much as some contemporary thinkers try to do; but what I have tentatively called "the movements" of Being in Heidegger's conception make it impossible to think of Being as something stable. The most important point of convergence, however, is the tension between meaning (i.e., that which makes things culturally specific), on the one hand, and presence or Being, on the other. It is true that only in the second of the two readings of "earth" and "world" that I have proposed do these two concepts correspond approximately to the idea of a tension between "presence" and "meaning." But the reason why I take some encouragement for my own project from concepts such as "earth," "world," or "Being" is independent of different interpretations of these concepts. Decisive for me is the general experience that they all—throughout their different interpretations—offer a degree of resistance to a smooth integration into any metaphysical worldview. Heidegger's concepts, it seems, are always already on the side of a departure into a different epistemological and ontological dimension.

4

One of my reasons for the decision to try and explore Heidegger's concept of "Being" came from the impression that it was no longer enough for us to state continually how tired we are in the humanities of a repertoire of analytic concepts that can only give us access to the dimension of meaning. In other words, once again, it is time to break certain discursive taboos (time to get one's hands dirty), time to develop concepts that can at least begin to grasp phenomena of presence, instead of just having to bypass this dimension (and to experiment with them). As I have already said several times in this book, the one strategy that can help us make progress here is the recourse to pre- or to nonmetaphysical cultures and discourses of the past. This exactly explains Heidegger's fascination with the texts of the pre-Socratics.[51] For sheer lack of expertise in the field of ancient Greek culture, I myself have used medieval culture, and the contrast between medieval and early modern culture, as a similar source of inspiration, and I shall now return to that material.

What I want to propose, then, based mainly on this specific historical contrast, are a number of concepts (they are hardly refined concepts so far) that might help us overcome the exclusive status of interpretation within the humanities (or that might at least help us imagine an intellectual situation where interpretation would no longer be exclusive). As these concepts are all taken from a contrastive description of medieval and (early) modern culture, I should perhaps say that they are meant to be, above all, illustrations of what it takes to imagine a culture fundamentally different from ours. Seen from this perspective, their alterity would no longer be a historically specific alterity. I shall produce and present these tentative concepts within two typologies. The first of these two typologies proposes a distinction between what I call "meaning culture" and "presence culture" (with meaning culture, of course, being close to modern culture and presence culture close to medieval culture).[52] As I know from long and sometimes frustrating experience that the implications of such typologies are often confused with those of reality descriptions, I insist that both the concept of "meaning culture" and that of "presence culture" should be understood as *Idealtypen*, in the tradition of Max Weber's sociology. I do not of course think that either of these *Idealtypen* has ever appeared (or will ever materialize) in its pure—in its ideal—form. Rather, I suppose that all cultures can be analyzed as complex configurations whose levels of self-reference bring together components of meaning culture and presence culture (as I claim that we can discover both meaning effects and presence effects in all cultural objects). Indeed, all the relevant conceptual and descriptive material that we can ever grasp from past cultures for such a kind of typology comes from their discourses of self-description. But despite our premise that all discourses of collective self-reference contain both meaning- and presence-culture elements, it makes sense to assume that some cultural phenomena (as, for example, the sacraments of the Catholic Church or the rationality of contemporary Afro-Brazilian cults) are more on the presence culture-side, whereas others (e.g., ancient Roman politics or the bureaucracy of the early modern Spanish Empire) are predominantly meaning-culture-based. Above all, one should not forget that this brief (and double) typology is meant to suggest the mere possibility of a not exclusively hermeneutic repertoire of concepts for cultural analysis.

First, the dominant human self-reference in a meaning culture is, then, the mind (we might also say consciousness or *res cogitans*), whereas the dominant self-reference in a presence culture is the body. *Second*, it is an implication of the mind being their dominant self-reference that humans conceive of themselves as eccentric in relation to the world (which is seen, in a meaning culture, as exclusively consisting of material objects). This view makes it obvious that it is "subjectivity" or "the subject" that occupies the place of the dominant human self-reference in a meaning culture whereas in presence cultures, humans consider their bodies to be part of a cosmology (or part of a divine creation). There, they don't see themselves as eccentric in relation to the world but as being part of the world (they are indeed in-the-world in a spatial and physical way). In a presence culture, the things of the world, on top of their material being, have an inherent meaning (not just a meaning conveyed to them through interpretation), and humans consider their bodies to be an integral part of their existence (hence, in late medieval society, the obsession with the theme of the bodily resurrection of the dead). *Third*, knowledge, in a meaning culture, can only be legitimate knowledge if it has been produced by a subject in an act of world-interpretation (and under the specific conditions of what I have, in the previous chapter, called "the hermeneutic field," that is, by penetrating the "purely material" surface of the world in order to find spiritual truth beneath or behind it). For a presence culture, legitimate knowledge is typically revealed knowledge. It is knowledge revealed by (the) god(s) or by different varieties of what one might describe as "events of self-unconceal-ment of the world." The impulse, as I said before, for such events of self-unconcealment never comes from the subject. Revelation and unconcealment, if you believe in them, just happen, and once they have happened, they can never be undone in their ef-fects. The "knowledge" that emerges from revelation and uncon-cealment does not necessarily and exclusively occur, however, in what we, in a predominantly meaning-based culture, think of as the only ontological way for knowledge to occur—that is, knowl-edge is not exclusively conceptual. Thinking along the lines of Heidegger's concept of Being should have encouraged us to imagine that "knowledge" revealed or unconcealed can be sub-stance that appears, that presents itself to us (even with its inher-ent meaning), without requiring interpretation as its transfor-mation into meaning.

These first three contrasts between aspects of meaning culture and aspects of presence culture make it plausible, *fourth*, that—explicitly or implicitly—they operate with different conceptions of what a sign must be. Of course, a sign in a meaning culture needs to have precisely the metaphysical structure that Ferdinand de Saussure contends is the universal condition of the sign: it is the coupling of a purely material signifier with a purely spiritual signified (or "meaning"). Now, it is important to add that, in a meaning culture, the "purely material" signifier ceases to be an object of attention as soon as its "underlying" meaning has been identified. A (for us) much less familiar form of the sign that the typological contrast between meaning culture and presence cul-ture can help us to further imagine and to grasp is close to the Aristotelian sign-definition that I have already explained, where a sign is a coupling between a substance (something that requires space) and a form (something that makes it possible for the sub-

stance to be perceived). This sign concept avoids the neat distinction between the purely spiritual and the purely material for
the two sides of what is brought together in the sign. Consequently, there is no side in this sign-concept that will vanish
once a meaning is secured. Without trying to ("culturally") over-
extend the range of the Aristotelian sign-concept here, I would
like to mention my memory of a Japanese tourist guide who first
gave me exact meanings, one by one, for the different rocks in a
famous stone garden—and then went on to add: "but these
stones are also beautiful because they keep on coming closer to
our bodies without ever pressing us." Such a world, a world
where stones keep on coming closer and where truth can be substance, that is, the world of presence culture, is a world where,
fifth, humans want to relate to the surrounding cosmology by inscribing themselves, that is, by inscribing their bodies, into the
rhythms of this cosmology. The will to derail or to alter such
rhythms (and even the unintentional accident of causing such a
change) is considered to be a sign of human fickleness or simply
a sin in a presence culture. In a meaning culture, in contrast,
humans tend to think of the transformation (of the improve-
ment, of the embellishment, etc.) of the world as their main vo-
cation. To imagine a world partly transformed through human
behavior is what we call a "motivation," and any behavior ori-
ented toward the realization of such imaginations is an "action."
Such visions of the future and such attempts at making them real
appear all the more legitimate the more they are based on hu-
man-produced knowledge of the world. What comes closest to
the meaning-culture concept of an "action" would in a presence
culture be the concept of "magic," that is, the practice of making
things that are absent present and things that are present absent.
Magic, however, never presents itself as based on humanly pro-

duced knowledge. Rather, it relies on recipes (often secret recipes or revealed recipes) whose content has been revealed to be a part of the never-changing movements in a cosmology of which humans consider themselves to be part. If the body is the dominant self-reference in a presence culture, then, *sixth*, space, that is, that dimension that constitutes itself around bodies, must be the primordial dimension in which the relationship between different humans and the relationship between humans and the things of the world are being negotiated. Time, in contrast, is the primordial dimension for any meaning culture, because there seems to be an unavoidable association between consciousness and temporality (think of Husserl's concept of the "stream of consciousness"). Above all, however, time is the primordial dimension of any meaning culture, because it takes time to carry out those transformative actions through which meaning cultures define the relationship between humans and the world. Now if space is the dominant dimension through which, in a presence culture, the relationship between humans, that is, between human bodies, is constituted, then this relationship, *seventh*, can constantly turn (and indeed tends to turn) into violence—that is, into occupying and blocking spaces with bodies—against other bodies. For meaning cultures, in contrast, it is typical (and perhaps even obligatory) to infinitely defer the moment of actual violence and to thus transform violence into power, which we can define as the potential of occupying or blocking spaces with bodies. The more the self-image of a certain culture corresponds to the typology of a meaning culture, the more it will try to hide and even to exclude violence as the ultimate potential of power. This is how we can explain the fact that, in recent decades, historians and philosophers of our culture have confused power relations with relations defined by the distribution of knowledge.

But the lines along which knowledge is distributed will only co-incide with the lines of power relations as long as the stability of the lines of knowledge distribution is ultimately covered, even in a meaning culture, by the potential and the threat of physical violence.

In a meaning culture, *eighth*, the concept of the event is in-separably linked to the value of innovation and, as its conse-quence, to the effect of surprise. In a presence culture, however, the equivalent of an innovation is the—necessarily illegitimate—departure from the regularities of a cosmology and its inherent codes of human conduct. This is why imagining a presence cul-ture implies the challenge of thinking a concept of eventness de-tached from innovation and surprise. Such a concept would re-mind us that even those regular changes and transformations that we can predict and expect imply a moment of discontinuity. We know that, shortly after eight o'clock in the evening, the or-chestra will begin to play an overture that we have heard many times. And yet the discontinuity that marks the moment in which the first sounds are produced will "hit" us—producing an effect of eventness that implies neither surprise nor innovation. The example of a stage-event brings us, *ninth*, to playfulness and fiction as concepts through which meaning cultures characterize interactions whose participants have a limited, a vague, or no awareness at all of the motivations that guide their behavior. This absence of (an awareness of) motivations that guide their behavior is the reason why, in situations of play or fiction, rules—either preexisting rules or rules that are being made up as the play unfolds—take over the place of the participants' moti-vations. With actions, defined as human behavior structured by conscious motivations, having no place in presence cultures, they cannot produce an equivalent of the concepts of playfulness or fiction—nor of the contrast between playfulness/fiction and the seriousness of everyday interactions.[53] If, in a meaning culture, the seriousness of everyday interactions finds an internal contrast in play and fiction, presence cultures need to suspend themselves—during sharply defined limits of time—whenever they want to allow for an exception from the cosmologically grounded rhythms of life. This is the structure that scholars inspired by Mikhail Bakhtin metonymically call "carnival."[54] *Finally*, to fill this very binary typology with some historical imagination, we could say, again, that parliamentary discussions are a ritual that fits for meaning cultures, whereas the Eucharist is a prototypical ritual for presence cultures. Parliamentary discussions, in principle, are a competition between different individual motivations, that is, between different visions of a remote future that can orient individual and collective behavior in an immediate future. Although parliamentary discussions, down to the present day, have counted on the physical presence of their participants, they stage themselves as being exclusively decided by the intellectual quality of the competing visions and arguments. The Eucharist, in contrast, is a ritual of magic because it makes God's body physically present as the central part of a past situation (as I said in the previous chapter, it was only early modern Protestant theology that turned the Eucharist into an act of commemoration). But what can be the point of a ritual that produces the real presence of God—if this real presence of God already is a generalized frame condition of human life? The only possible answer is that the celebration of the Eucharist, day after day, will not only maintain but intensify the already existing real presence of God. The concept of intensification makes us understand that it is not unusual, for presence cultures, to quantify what would not be available for quantification in a meaning culture: presence cultures do quantify feelings, for example, or the impressions of closeness and absence, or the degrees of approval and resistance.[55]

It belongs to the inherent possibilities of such typologies that they allow for almost endless continuation and refinement, and because the ten contrasts noted appear to be a random enough number, I conclude the binary typology of "presence cultures" and "meaning cultures" here. I would like to finish this chapter, dedicated to various attempts at imagining a relationship to texts, to cultural objects, and to the world at large that is not an exclusively interpretative relation, with yet another typology. Instead of trying to complexify conceptions of different types of culture, this second typology focuses on different types of human world-appropriation (with the concept of "world" including other humans). Instead of being binary, our second typology distinguishes between four different types of world-appropriation. The order in which I shall present these four different types of world-appropriation can be explained as moving from a mode of world-appropriation that would correspond to an ideal type of presence culture toward the opposite polarity, that is, that of pure meaning culture. What will not change between my first and my second typology is their argumentative function. As I did in my development of the concepts of "presence culture" and "meaning culture," I shall now distinguish four different types of world-appropriation, again in the ultimate hope of suggesting and inspiring images and concepts that might help us grasp noninterpretative components in our relationship to the world.[56]

Eating the things of the world, including the practices of anthropophagy and theophagy, "chewing Madame Bovary,"[57] as Friedrich Nietzsche once imagined, or eating the body and drinking the blood of Christ, all belong to one obvious and crucial mode of world-appropriation—a crucial mode of world-appropriation, however, about which we don't like to talk and that we constantly struggle to project toward and, above all, beyond the margins of our own meaning culture. The most obvious reason for this not only intellectual antipathy is, of course, the tension between our culture as predominantly meaning-centered, on the one hand, and, on the other hand, eating the world as the most direct way of becoming one with the things of the world in their tangible presence. But perhaps there is yet another mechanism intervening in this reaction, a mechanism for which we shall find equivalents in the three other types of world-appropriation. For in each type of world-appropriation those who are the agents of appropriating the world experience the fear of becoming the objects of the same type of appropriation. Eating the world, then, will always trigger the fear, for humans as bodily parts of the world, that they might themselves be eaten. And this is precisely why most human societies make the eating of human flesh taboo, whether a general taboo or a taboo against eating the flesh of one's own kin.

Penetrating things and bodies—that is, body contact and sexuality, aggression, destruction,[58] and murder—constitute a second type of world appropriation, in which the merging of bodies with other bodies or with inanimate things is always transitory and therefore necessarily opens up a space of distance for desire and for reflection. This, I think, is the context that explains why sexuality allows for such a strong connotation of death, of overwhelming another body or of being overwhelmed by it. As a longing for death, this connotation may come from the desire to make a transitory union eternal. But as a fear of death, it seems to be triggered, once again, by a fear of reversal. Fear of violent penetration may produce the nightmare of being raped. There are multiple cultural arrays to cope with this fear.

In some cultures, a strict distribution and hierarchization of sexual roles tries to sever the right to penetrate from the threat of being penetrated. A seemingly much more "civilized"—or, to use a concept from a long-faded intellectual discourse, a much more alienating—strategy of deflecting this fear is, of course, the habit, almost generally accepted in our own culture, of spiritualizing sexuality up to a point where it turns into mutual self-expression and communication.

There is a mode of world-appropriation in which, on the one hand, the presence of the world or of the other is still physically felt although, on the other hand, there is no perception of a real object that would account for this feeling. This is what we call *mysticism*. It is interesting, within this typology, that our culture categorizes all forms of mysticism as forms of spiritual life—which leaves as a problem the double experience that states of mystical rapture are often induced by highly ritualized body practices and always come with the perception of a physical impact. Of course, the desire of which mysticism allows full awareness is still a desire of lasting possession—a possession of the things of the world, of the beloved one, of a god. But mysticism, too, may turn into the fear of being possessed and that means, as we can relate mysticism with an at least rudimentarily developed subject position among its practitioners, that it is related with the fear of permanently losing control over oneself. It is this specific fear that has obliged most of the famous mystics to dedicate long and complicated reflections to the question of which preventions and mechanisms might guarantee the possibility of returning from a state of mystical possession. More interesting, perhaps, and certainly much more radical, is the opposite strategy of deliberately opening oneself to a violent act of being possessed by a god. In this case, which is the case of the so-called *pais do santo* ("fathers of the gods/saints") in most Afro-Brazilian cults, it seems to be the desire to be possessed, turned into a full-fledged intention and strategy of being possessed, that deflects the fear of being overwhelmed.

Of course, *interpretation* and *communication* as exclusively spiritual ways of world-appropriation correspond to the meaning-culture pole in this typology. Every effort to think and to show that this is not the only way of referring to and appropriating the things of the world is a potential step beyond the exclusivity of the meaning dimension. But if, at this point, there were still a need to evoke or even to describe, in this context, the standard implications of interpretation and communication, this book would have been pointless. So we can immediately turn to the specific fear produced by what we might want to call "total communication." This is, of course, the fear of being accessible, in one's innermost thoughts and feelings, of being accessible and open like a book to the interpretative cunning of parents and teachers, of spouses and intelligence agents. There is a ritual to deflect this fear which, in its basic structures, corresponds exactly to the deliberate openness of the *pai do santo* to the act of possession by a god. Its equivalent in a communication culture is psychoanalysis and psychotherapy. Could it not be that, more than the result of being read, what really matters in psychoanalysis is overcoming the fear of being read—by deliberately opening oneself and by even paying handsome amounts of money in order to make happen what one most fears. The complementary strategy is the art of feigning, the art of hiding one's innermost thoughts and feelings behind the mask of an "expression" that does not express anything.[59] This, as I already mentioned, is the art that convinced Machiavelli that the Catholic King Fernando de Aragón was the first incarnation of the modern politician. The most perfect way of hiding behind a mask is to be absolutely silent. And silence connects with the muteness of things present with the muteness that produces their presence. There is no emergence of meaning, on the other hand, that does not alleviate the weight of presence.

Epiphany/Presentification/Deixis:
Futures for the Humanities and Arts

1

Let us now take a moment to see how much ground we have covered so far—before we concentrate on the future. For just as Moses was not allowed to have more than a look into the promised land, we are not able yet (for sheer lack of appropriate concepts) to enter an intellectual world of postmetaphysical epistemology—and this explains why it matters to know at least what exactly we have left behind ourselves. Derrida was right: overcoming metaphysics is certainly an uphill struggle. Less so because it is hard to forget a specific past, however, than because it requires both imagination and stamina to conquer the potential concepts of a nonmetaphysical future. At any event, instead of indulging with Derrida in the soft paradox of a situation that we do not want to bring to an "end," although its "closure is outlined," I would like to adopt the deparadoxifying attitude of those who trade in "futures"—that is, in "commodities or stocks bought or sold upon agreement of delivery in time to come"[1]— and act as if an agreement of delivery had already been signed.

This chapter, then, is about possible (but not yet definitely conquered) intellectual and institutional "futures," about possible future practices in the academic disciplines that we subsume under the name of "the humanities and arts." But it is also, of course, written with the (mostly implicit) acknowledgment that the "delivery" of such "futures" has not yet happened (or cannot really happen), and before trying to offer a more or less panoramic view of the promised land, it therefore starts with a look back.

This book began with academic memories from the late 1970s and the 1980s, memories of that (now strangely) "heroic" intention to keep alive a "theory debate" in the humanities that had begun a decade and a half earlier, in the mid and late 1960s, and that seemed to be petering out about a quarter of a century ago. The very good intention of keeping up that "theory debate," like most good intentions, produced quite an amount of boredom and repetition, but it also generated at least one prospect that looked immediately exciting to us, that is, the prospect of focusing on "materialities of communication." Trying to figure out how one could possibly define "materialities of communication" and what the most adequate tools for their analysis would be, we found ourselves obliged to think of the humanities, as they then existed (and as they still predominantly exist), as an epistemological tradition that, for more than a century, had separated us from everything that could not be described as or transformed into a configuration of meaning. Today, we may add that it was most probably the trauma inflicted by this—hermeneutically induced—"loss of world" that explains why the only value (at least the highest value) that many humanists can find in the phenomena they are dealing with is the motivation to enter yet another intellectual loop of "self-reflexivity," and this is probably also the reason why adopting anything but a "critical" attitude toward the things of the worlds in which we are living seems to be something like an original sin, at least in the eyes of the average humanist.

In contrast, trying to establish a position within the humanities and arts that could mark an exception to their century-old tradition of being an institution in which hermeneutics and self-reflexivity are the law (and from being an extension, into our present, of what I have been referring to as the "metaphysical" tradition), thus breaking away from the currently dominant self-understanding of the humanities and arts and from the practices based on that self-understanding, appeared to be the one worth-while next step to take. It then became the double experience of this book's previous (and third) chapter that, above all, there was no way of even getting close to the goal of leaving the metaphysical tradition behind (or at least of modifying it in a serious way) without going further and breaking several taboos that threatened and still threaten to be borders of intellectual bad taste; and that, even after breaking these taboos (and after "getting our hands dirty"), it was still quite a laborious undertaking to imagine and conquer any conceptual terrain that deserves to be called "nonhermeneutic."

Now, what could the promise of a disciplinary future based on a new epistemology look like? Of course, one should anticipate that all the borders of the humanistic disciplines, such as we have known them, would have to be redrawn. But as so many predictions about how exactly they might be redrawn have turned out to be (sometimes awkwardly) wrong in the past, and as my interest in the future here is an interest in intellectual practices, rather than in disciplinary maps, I shall rely, in this chapter, on a very traditional tripartition that has been and still is operational in many (although obviously not all) humanistic disciplines. I am referring to the hearteningly unsophisticated and largely self-explanatory tripartition of these disciplines into "aesthetics," "history," and "pedagogy." Of course, these three fields were never supposed to belong to the same level of practice and abstraction or to be mutually independent—which doubly negative premise has inspired endless proposals to rethink their interrelationship. In my own very tender academic youth, for example, I imagined (together with many German humanists of my generation, I suppose) that the historical study of cultural artifacts would invariably help us to appreciate and understand their aesthetic value; that aesthetic value invariably lay in the potential of conveying an ethical message; and that therefore, and depending largely on the ethical insights that they provided, the relative aesthetico-ethical value of whatever texts or works of art we were teaching would indeed establish a basic pedagogical orientation for us.[2]

The way in which I understand the relationship between the fields of aesthetics, history, and pedagogy has changed quite dramatically as a consequence, not only of the growing importance that reflection on "presence" has had in my work, but of serious doubts—my own included[3]—about both the commensurability of aesthetic experience and ethical norms and the possible role of ethical orientation in academic teaching in general. Above all, I would refrain, today, from lining up these areas or subfields in any inductive or deductive order. If I had to give priority to one of them (although I do not see any urgent need to do so), I would probably pick aesthetics, because of the specific epistemological relevance inherent to the type of *epiphany* that it can provide—without claiming, however, that exclusively aesthetic experience is capable of producing such an epiphany.[4] What most interests me today in the field of history, the *presentification* of past worlds—that is, techniques that produce the impression (or, rather, the illusion) that worlds of the past can become tangible again—is an activity without any explanatory power in relation to the relative values of different forms of aesthetic experience (providing such explanations is what we used to think of as the function of historical knowledge in relation to aesthetics). But as the new conception of the field of history shares with the field of aesthetics the distinctive presence-component, and as it does not pretend to offer any immediate ethical or even "political" orientation, the program of presentification lends itself to the traditional accusation of promoting an "aestheticization of history." My first line of defense would simply be to ask back what at all could be wrong with such an aestheticization of history. Regarding the field of teaching, finally, I have convinced myself, over the past few years, that neither aesthetic nor historical experience (at least aesthetic and historical experience as I see them) dispose of any potential that would yield superior orientation for behavior and action on the individual or on the collective level. Moreover, I doubt whether providing such orientation should really be a function of our teaching, at least on the academic level, even if it were readily available. Rather, I am convinced that it is our preeminent task today to confront students with intellectual complexity, which means that *deictic gestures*—that is, pointing to occasional condensations of such complexity—are what we should really focus on.

Epiphany, presentification, and *deixis,* then, would be three tentative concepts in which I try to bring together my predictions, imaginings, and desires about future forms of practice in the humanities and the arts. In this context, I want the component of "the arts" to play a much more prominent role than that of merely being a traditional part within the name for a cluster of academic disciplines. For I believe that, in their convergence, the moves of putting more emphasis on the presence element in aesthetic experience; the potential aestheticization of history; and the proposal to liberate our teaching from the obligation of providing ethical orientation may create, once again, a greater awareness of how close to actual artistic practice some of our academic activities can be. But while I will have to admit that I myself am not able to live and to exemplify this potential closeness between the humanities and the arts, neither in my own professional everyday activities nor through the following, more detailed illustrations of how I imagine the fields of aesthetics, history, and teaching to develop, I hope that I shall at least manage to keep awake the claim for their new proximity. Finally, I should also announce that the three parts of this chapter will not be of equal length. The most detailed conceptual development will be dedicated to the dimension of aesthetics. This is because I think that the part on aesthetics will contain certain arguments that may be foundational for my conceptions of historicization and of teaching, too. But it will also and simply be the case because this is the first time that I have tried to produce a written version of my thinking on aesthetics, whereas I have already published such texts on the fields of history and of teaching.[5]

2

When, a few years ago, a young colleague from the musicology department at Stanford and I were invited to teach an obligatory "Introduction to the Humanities" course for about two hundred students of the incoming freshman class, and when we had first decided on the general topic and task of exposing our prospective students to different types of *aesthetic experience*,[6] three implications were uncontroversial between us right from the start. We just wanted to point to different modalities of enjoying beautiful things, without making aesthetic experience an obligation for our students (in other words, we wanted to offer them an opportunity to find out whether they reacted positively to the potential of aesthetic experience, and, if so, we wanted to let them discover which modalities of aesthetic experience they preferred); secondly, we did not try to argue in favor of aesthetic experience by alluding to any values beyond the intrinsic feeling of intensity that it can trigger; and, finally, we wanted to open the range of potential objects of aesthetic experience by transgressing the canon of their traditional forms (such as "literature," "classical music," "avant-garde painting," etc.). This move was carried by the conviction that, today, the field where aesthetic experience actually takes place must be far more extended than what the concept "aesthetic experience" covers.

My *first* more personal concern for this class was to be a good enough teacher to evoke for my students and to make them feel specific *moments of intensity* that I remember with fondness and mostly with nostalgia—even if, in some cases, this intensity was painful when it actually happened. I wanted my students to know, for example, the almost excessive, exuberant sweetness that sometimes overcomes me when a Mozart aria grows into polyphonic complexity and when I indeed believe that I can hear the tones of the oboe on my skin. I want my students to live or at least to imagine that moment of admiration (and perhaps also of the despair of an aging man) that gets a hold of me when I see the beautiful body of a young woman standing next to me in front of one of the computers that give access to our library catalogue—a moment, by the way, that is not all that different from the joy that I feel when the quarterback of my favorite college team in American football (Stanford Cardinal of course) stretches out his perfectly sculpted arms to celebrate a touchdown pass. Quite naturally, I also want all of my students to feel the elation, the suddenly very deep breathing and the embarrassingly wet eyes with which I must have reacted to that very beautifully executed pass and to the swift movement of the wide receiver who caught it. I hope that some of my students will suffer through that sentiment of intense depression and perhaps even of humiliation that I know from reading "Pequeño vals vienés," my favorite poem in Federico García Lorca's *Poeta en Nueva York*, a text that makes the reader intuit how the life of a homosexual man was emotionally and even physically amputated in Western societies around 1930. My students should get at least a glimpse of that illusion of lethal empowerment and violence, as if I (of all people!) were an ancient god, which permeates my body at the moment of the *estocada final* in a Spanish bullfight, when the bullfighter's sword silently cuts through the body of the bull, and the bull's muscles seem to stiffen for a moment— before its massive body breaks down like a house shaken by an earthquake. I want my students to join in that promise of an endlessly and eternally quiet world that sometimes seems to surround me when I get lost in front of a painting by Edward Hopper. I hope they experience the explosion of tasty nuances that comes with the first bite of great food. And I want them to know the feeling of having found the right place for one's body with which a perfectly designed building can embrace and welcome us.

There is nothing edifying in such moments, no message, nothing that we could really learn from them—and this is why I like to refer to them as "moments of intensity." For what we feel is probably not more than a specifically high level in the functioning of some of our general cognitive, emotional, and perhaps even physical faculties. The difference that these moments make seems to be based in quantity. And I like to combine the quantitative concept of "intensity" with the meaning of temporal fragmentation in the word "moments" because I know—from

many and mostly frustrating moments of loss and of separation—that there is no reliable, no guaranteed way of producing
moments of intensity, and that we have even less hope of holding
on to them or extending their duration. Indeed, I cannot be sure,
before I hear my favorite Mozart aria, whether that exuberant
sweetness will overcome my body again. It might happen—but I
know and I already anticipate my reaction of regret about this
experience—that it will only happen for a moment (if it should
happen at all).

ᔐ

But how is it possible that we long for such moments of intensity
although they have no edifying contents or effects to offer? Why
do we sometimes remember them as happy moments and sometimes as sad moments—but always with a feeling of loss or of
nostalgia? This is the *second* question that I want to deal with,
the question *of the specific appeal that such moments hold for us*,
the question about the reasons that motivate us to seek aesthetic
experience and to expose our bodies and minds to its potential.
Without going into any detail yet, my opening hypothesis is that
what we call "aesthetic experience" always provides us with certain feelings of intensity that we cannot find in the historically
and culturally specific everyday worlds that we inhabit. This is
why, seen from a historical or from a sociological perspective,
aesthetic experience can indeed function as a symptom of the
preconscious needs and desires that belong to specific societies.[7]
But I do not want to equate the motivational power of such desires, which may draw us into situations of aesthetic experience,
on the one hand, with the interpretation and understanding of
that motivational power as based in preconscious desires, on the
other. In other words, I do not believe that such interpretations

and the higher degree of self-reflexivity that might follow from them should be considered a part of aesthetic experience. For the same reason, I prefer to speak, as often as possible, of "moments of intensity" or of "lived experience" (*ästhetisches Erleben*) instead of saying "aesthetic experience" (*ästhetische Erfahrung*)—because most philosophical traditions associate the concept of "experience" with interpretation, that is, with acts of meaning attribution. When I use the concepts *Erleben* or "lived experience," in contrast, I mean them in the strict sense of the phenomenological tradition, namely, as a being focused upon, as a thematizing of, certain objects of lived experience (objects that offer specific degrees of intensity under our own cultural conditions— whenever we call them "aesthetic"). Lived experience or *Erleben* presupposes that purely physical perception (*Wahrnehmung*) has already taken place, on the one hand, and that it will be followed by experience (*Erfahrung*) as the result of acts of world interpretation, on the other.

Now, if what fascinates us in moments of aesthetic experience,[8] if what attracts us without being accompanied by a clear awareness of the reasons for this attraction, is always something that our everyday worlds are not capable of offering us; and if we further presuppose that our everyday worlds are historically and culturally specific, then it follows that the objects of aesthetic experience, too, must be culturally specific. Regarding the other side of the situation whose structures I try to describe, it is not clear to me whether, for the readers, spectators, and listeners who are attracted by those historically specific objects of aesthetic experience, we have to presuppose a corresponding historicity in their forms of aesthetic experience. But I do not believe that it is absolutely necessary to resolve this very large question as long as we are dealing with aesthetic experience in the context of trying to imagine future intellectual practices for the humanities and arts. For it is my impression that if those forms of reaction and of reception undergo profound changes at all, the pace of such transformations must be much slower than the pace at which the objects of aesthetic experience are changing. What I have said so far implies, in addition, that we shall not—and perhaps should not—limit our analysis of aesthetic experience to the side of the recipient and to the mental (and perhaps also physical) invest- ments that he (or she) may make. For it appears that these in- vestments and their yield will depend, at least partly, on the ob- jects of fascination by which they are first activated and evoked. This is one of the reasons why it matters, for a general descrip- tion of aesthetic experience, to deal with these objects— although, perhaps, the comparatively fast pace of their historical transformation makes them resistant to integration into any gen- eral theory.

◡

If aesthetic experience is always evoked by and if it always refers to moments of intensity that cannot be part of the respective ev- eryday worlds in which it takes place, then it follows that aes- thetic experience will be necessarily located at a certain distance from these everyday worlds. This very obvious conclusion brings us to a *third* layer in the analysis of aesthetic experience, namely, to the *situational framework within which it typically occurs.* As a central feature of this situational framework, the distance be- tween aesthetic experience and everyday worlds is one possible reference for the explanation of the double isolation inherent in all moments of aesthetic intensity, and this is the double iso- lation that Karl Heinz Bohrer has so impressively described through the concepts of "suddenness" and "farewell." There is,

on the one hand, no systematic, no pedagogically guaranteed
way of leading students (or other victims of good pedagogical
intentions) "toward" aesthetic experience; on the other hand,
there is no predictable, obvious or typical yield that aesthetic experience can add to our lives in the everyday worlds. For the general description of this situational condition, I want to use the
concept of "insularity" that Mikhail Bakhtin has developed in
his analysis of the culture of carnival. For "insularity" seems to
carry less historically specific connotations than the concept of
"aesthetic autonomy"—in which the distance from the everyday
is already interpreted as a gain of subjective independence. I
therefore propose to reserve the name "aesthetic autonomy" for
the specific forms that the general structural condition of "insularity" developed during the eighteenth and nineteenth centuries. This, of course, assumes that the insularity of aesthetic experience existed long before the eighteenth century and that it also
has a place outside Western culture.

The most important consequence that follows from the insularity of aesthetic experience is the incommensurability between
aesthetic experience and the institutional propagation of ethical
norms—and this seems to be a central issue in Bohrer's reflection
on "aesthetic negativity" too.[9] For ethical norms are—and
should be—part of historically specific everyday worlds, whereas
we have postulated that aesthetic experience draws its fascination
(in the literal sense of the word) from offering moments of intensity that cannot be a part of specific everyday worlds. It therefore
makes sense to say that the combination of aesthetics with ethics,
that is, the projection of ethical norms on to the potential objects
of aesthetic experience, will inevitably lead to the erosion of the
potential intensity of the latter. In other words, to adapt aesthetic
intensity to ethical requirements means to normalize and ulti-

mately dilute it. Whenever conveying or exemplifying an ethical message is supposed to be the main function of a work of art, we need to ask—and indeed the question cannot be eliminated—whether it would not be more efficient to articulate that same ethical message in rather straightforward and explicit concepts and forms.

～

My *fourth* reflection refers to a *specific disposition* that I believe goes along, quite regularly, with the structural condition of "insularity." There are two principal ways of entering situations of insularity. The more dramatic one (so to speak) is the modality of being caught by "imposed upon relevance" (*auferlegte Relevanz*).[10] There, the sudden appearance of certain objects of perception diverts our attention from ongoing everyday routines and indeed temporarily separates us from them. Nature turned into an event often fulfills this function: think of lightning, above all, the first lightning in a thunderstorm, or remember the aggressive sunlight that almost blinds you when, coming from central Europe, you deplane at any Californian destination. Charles Baudelaire's poem "À une passante" is a literary staging of the imposed upon relevance of a female body that catches and almost overwhelms the idle flaneur's attention. Such eventness is certainly different from a classroom situation where we try to facilitate the happening of aesthetic appearance, although fully aware that no pedagogical effort will ever guarantee the coming of the actual experience. But we can point to the presence of certain objects of experience and invite our students to be composed,[11] that is, to be both open and concentrated, without letting such concentration harden into the tension of an effort.

The best description that I know for the moment when the

composed disposition that prepares us for the happening of aesthetic experience turns into actual aesthetic experience comes from an athlete. It was the answer that Pablo Morales, an Olympic gold medalist in swimming, gave to the question of why, after having retired from competitive sports, he had come back to qualify for the Olympics again and to win yet another gold medal. Without hesitation, Morales replied that he had made this astonishing effort because he was addicted to the feeling of "being lost in focused intensity."[12] His choice of the word "intensity" confirms that the difference that aesthetic experience makes is, above all, a difference of quantity: extreme challenges produce extreme levels of performance in our minds and our bodies. That Morales wanted to be "lost" corresponds to the structural element of insularity, to the element of distance vis-à-vis the everyday world that belongs to the situation of aesthetic experience. Finally, Morales called the intensity that attracts him "focused"—which seems to indicate that the disposition of composed openness anticipates the energizing presence of an object of experience to come. Now, what Morales was talking about was the challenge of participating in athletic competition on a world-class level. Some people might have reservations about subsuming such situations of competition under a concept of "aesthetic experience." But even then the question remains of what general features we can identify in those objects of experience—aesthetic or not—that attract us and push us to the state of being lost in focused intensity.

෴

This precisely is my *fifth* question, and perhaps the most obviously relevant, the decisive question in this context: *what is it that fascinates us in the objects of aesthetic experience?* From our

second reflection, it is clear that whatever features we may identify in the object of aesthetic experience, the status of our answers will be historically specific—even if, on the side of experience, the pace of historical transformation may be extremely
slow. In searching for the always more or less hidden desire that
could motivate us to transcend our contemporary everyday
worlds (which, of course, also means that we are looking for everyday phenomena and conditions with which we are overly
saturated), I do not know of a more convincing answer than the
one given by Jean-Luc Nancy in his book *The Birth to Presence,*
in the opening pages of which he argues that there is nothing we
find more tiresome today than the production of yet another nu-
ance of meaning, of just "a little more sense."[13] What in contrast
we miss in a world so saturated with meaning, and what therefore turns into a primary object of (not fully conscious) desire in
our culture, are—very unsurprisingly by now, in the context of
my book, I admit (and I hope)—phenomena and impressions of
presence.

Presence and meaning always appear together, however, and
are always in tension. There is no way of making them compati-
ble or of bringing them together in one "well-balanced" phe-
nomenal structure. I do not want to go into a comparison and
detailed discussion of different philosophical definitions of
"meaning" and/or "sense" (there always seem to be too many of
them anyway)—but I understand that what makes meaning,
that is, the awareness of a choice that has taken place (or the
awareness of possible alternatives to what has been chosen), is
the very dimension of consciousness that is denied by the type of
physical presence for which we are longing, or that simply does
not come into play. That glaring sunlight or that lightning,
when they hit me, are not experienced as "the other" of a less

luminous day or of thunder. Typologically speaking, the dimension of meaning is dominant in Cartesian worlds, in worlds for which consciousness (the awareness of alternatives) constitutes the core of human self-reference. And are we not precisely longing for presence, is our desire for tangibility not so intense—because our own everyday environment is so almost insuperably consciousness-centered? Rather than having to think, always and endlessly, what else there could be, we sometimes seem to connect with a layer in our existence that simply wants the things of the world close to our skin.

Now Jean-Luc Nancy does not only (and simply) point to this very layer of a desire for presence that reacts to specific conditions in our contemporary culture. He also observes—and this indeed is why he emphasizes the double movement of a "birth to presence" and a "vanishing of presence"—that those presence effects that we can live are always already permeated with absence. From an only slightly different conceptual angle, we could rephrase Nancy's point by saying that, for us, presence phenomena cannot help being inevitably ephemeral, cannot help being what I call "effects of" presence—because we can only encounter them within a culture that is predominantly a meaning culture. For us, presence phenomena always come as "presence effects" because they are necessarily surrounded by, wrapped into, and perhaps even mediated by clouds and cushions of meaning. It is extremely difficult—if not impossible—for us *not* to "read," not to try and attribute meaning to that lightning or to that glaring California sunlight. This may well have been the reason why Heidegger became so obsessed with (and so conceptually entangled in) the duplicity of and the relationship between "earth" and "world" in his essay "The Origin of the Work of Art." My own (modest) reaction to these observations, my answer to the question regarding the specific features that mark the objects of aesthetic experience is, then, to say that objects of aesthetic experience (and here it becomes important, once again, to insist that I am speaking of "lived experience," of *Erleben*) are characterized by an oscillation between presence effects and meaning effects. While it may be true, in principle, that all of our (human) relationships to the things of the world must be both meaning- and presence-based relations, I still claim that, under contemporary cultural conditions, we need a specific framework (namely, the situation of "insularity" and the disposition of "focused intensity") in order to really experience (*erleben*) the productive tension, the oscillation between meaning and presence—instead of just bracketing the presence side, as we seem to do, quite automatically, in our so very Cartesian everyday lives. I think (and I hope, of course) that my thesis about the oscillation between presence effects and meaning effects is close to what Hans-Georg Gadamer meant when he emphasized that, in addition to their apophantic dimension, that is, in addition to the dimension that can and must be redeemed through interpretation, poems have a "volume"—a dimension, that is, that demands our voice, that needs to be "sung."[14] I also suppose (and again hope) that my conclusion converges with Niklas Luhmann's thesis according to which the "art system" is the only social system in which perception (in the phenomenological meaning of a human relationship to the world mediated by the senses) is not only a precondition of system-intrinsic communication but also, together with meaning, part of what this communication carries.[15]

What Luhmann highlights as a specific feature of the art system is a simultaneity of meaning and perception, of meaning effects and presence effects—and if this is not too much of a subject-centered perspective to be applied to Luhmann's philosophy,

I would venture to say that what he found to be specific to the art system may well be the possibility to experience (*erleben*) meaning effects and presence effects in simultaneity. Whenever it presents itself to us, we may live this simultaneity as a tension or as an oscillation. Essential is the point that, within this specific constellation, meaning will not bracket, will not make the presence effects disappear, and that the—unbracketed—physical presence of things (of a text, of a voice, of a canvas with colors, of a play performed by a team) will not ultimately repress the meaning dimension. Nor is the relation between presence effects and meaning effects a relation of complementarity, in which a function assigned to each side in relation to the other would give the co-presence of the two sides the stability of a structural pattern. Rather, we can say that the tension/oscillation between presence effects and meaning effects endows the object of aesthetic experience with a component of provocative instability and unrest.

There is a rule, a prescription, a convention in Argentinian culture that very beautifully illustrates why I am emphasizing so much this noncomplementarity in the relationship between presence effects and meaning effects.[16] In Argentina, you are not supposed to dance a tango that has lyrics—although the often striking literary quality of tango lyrics has long constituted an object of legitimate cultural pride. The rationality behind this convention seems to be that, within a nonbalanced situation of simultaneity between meaning effects and presence effects, paying attention to the lyrics of a tango would make it very difficult to follow the rhythm of the music with one's body; and such divided attention would probably make it next to impossible that one let go, that one—quite literally—"let fall" one's body into the rhythm of this music, which is certainly necessary for whoever wants to execute the very complex steps of the tango, that is, the forms of a dance whose female and male choreographies are never coordinated before the actual performance begins. In other words—and this is an exact example of what I mean when I speak of a "tension" or an "oscillation" between presence effects and meaning effects: whoever tries to capture the semantic complexity that makes tango lyrics so melancholic, will deprive herself of the full pleasure that may come from a fusion between the tango movement and her body. And as I have no specific interest in arguing for a dominance of presence effects over meaning effects, it may be good to emphasize that the opposite is also true: while they are dancing, even the most perfect tango performers cannot fully grasp the semantic complexity of tango lyrics.

In saying that every human contact with the things of the world contains both a meaning- and a presence-component, and that the situation of aesthetic experience is specific inasmuch as it allows us to live both these components in their tension, I do not mean to imply that the relative weight of these two components will always be equal. On the contrary, I assume that there are always specific distributions between the meaning-component and the presence-component—which depend on the materiality (i.e., on the mediatic modality) of each object of aesthetic experience. For example, the meaning-dimension will always be dominant when we are reading a text—but literary texts have ways of also bringing the presence-dimension of the typography, of the rhythm of language, and even of the smell of paper into play. Conversely, I believe that the presence dimension will always dominate when we are listening to music—and at the same time it is true that certain musical structures can evoke certain semantic connotations. But however minimal the participation

of one or the other dimension may become under specific mediatic conditions, I think that aesthetic experience—at least in
our culture—will always confront us with the tension, or oscillation, between presence and meaning. This is the reason why an
exclusively semiotic (in my terminology, exclusively metaphysical) concept of the sign cannot do justice to aesthetic experience.
We need, on the one hand, a semiotic sign-concept to describe
and to analyze its meaning-dimension. But, on the other hand,
we also need a different sign-concept—the Aristotelian coupling
of "substance" and "form," for example—for the presence-
dimension in aesthetic experience. And if it is true, as I have argued, that the two dimensions will never grow into a stable
structure of complementarity, then we must understand that it is
not only unnecessary but indeed analytically counterproductive
to try and develop a combination, a complex metaconcept fusing
the semiotic and nonsemiotic definitions of the sign.

One might object that this juxtaposition of two types of sign-
concepts that will not be brought together in a semantic structure of higher complexity is a symptom of failure; more precisely,
one could say that it proves that we have not yet really overcome
the ontological duplicity characteristic of metaphysics. From a
certain perspective, from the perspective of a truly new epistemology, for which we may long, I have no major objection to
such an objection. On the other hand, however, my answer to
the question of what it is that fascinates us in situations of aesthetic experience was meant to be a historically specific answer.
The desire for presence that I have invoked is a reaction to an
overly Cartesian, historically specific everyday world that we at
least sometimes wish to overcome. It is thus neither surprising
nor embarrassing that in this context—that is, in our own historical situation—the conceptual tools with which we try to

analyze the traces of this desire for presence, in their environment charged with meaning, are also partly meaning- and partly presence-oriented.

꙳

I shall now concentrate, as a *sixth* step of my argument, on the specific mode in which the oscillation between presence effects and meaning effects presents itself to us in situations of aesthetic experience. *Epiphany* is the notion that I want to use and unfold in this context.[17] By "epiphany," I am not referring again to the simultaneity, tension, and oscillation between meaning and presence but, above all, to the feeling, mentioned and theorized by Jean-Luc Nancy, that we cannot hold on to those presence effects, that they—and with them the simultaneity between presence and meaning—are ephemeral. More precisely, I want to comment, under the heading of "epiphany," on three features that shape the way in which the tension between presence and meaning presents itself to us: on the impression that the tension between presence and meaning, when it occurs, comes out of nothing; on the emergence of this tension as having a spatial articulation; on the possibility of describing its temporality as an "event."

If we assume (as indeed I have) that there is no aesthetic experience without a presence effect, and no presence effect without substance in play; if we further assume that a substance in order to be perceived needs a form; and if we finally assume (as I also have in the previous reflection) that the presence-component in the tension or oscillation that constitutes aesthetic experience can never be held stable, then it follows that whenever an object of aesthetic experience emerges and momentarily produces in us that feeling of intensity, it seems to come out of nothing. For no such substance and form were present to us before. With certain ontological implications that I find fascinating but that one does not necessarily have to accept in order to agree with his description, Heidegger makes exactly this point: "*Art then is the becoming and happening of truth.* Does truth, then, arise out of nothing? It does indeed if by nothing is meant the mere not of that which is, and if we here think of that which is as an object present in the ordinary way."[18]

As that which seems to emerge out of nothing has a substance and a form, it is unavoidable for its epiphany to require a spatial dimension (or at least an impression thereof). This is another motif in Heidegger's "Origin of the Work of Art," mainly developed in relation to the concept "earth" and in the famous passage about the Greek temple: "The temple's firm towering makes visible the invisible space of the air. The steadfastness of the work contrasts with the surge of the surf, and its own repose brings out the raging of the sea. Tree and grass, eagle and bull, snake and cricket first enter into their distinctive shapes and come to appear as what they are. The Greeks called this emerging and rising in itself and in all things *phusis.* It clears and illuminates, also, that on which and in which man bases his dwelling. We call this ground the *earth.*"[19] Within Western culture, we find a particular sense of this spatial dimension of epiphany in Calderón's drama, specifically in the genre of the *auto sacramental* whose performance was reserved to the day of Corpus Christi, the Church holiday that celebrates the Eucharist. Calderón's scenographic instructions abound with dispositions for material forms to "emerge," to "rise," or to "vanish," and for bodies to "come close" to the spectators and then to "recede." Likewise, in No and Kabuki, the traditional staging forms of Japanese theater, the spatial dimension of epiphany seems to be the central element of the performance. All actors come to the stage across a bridge that cuts through the audience, and as a complicated choreography of steps back and forth, this coming to the stage often occupies more time (and more attention among the spectators) than the actors' actual play on the stage.

Finally, there are three aspects that give the epiphany-component within aesthetic experience the status of an event. In the first place (and I have already mentioned this condition earlier on), we never know whether or when such an epiphany will occur. Secondly, if it occurs, we do not know what form it will take and how intense it will be: there are no two bolts of lightning, indeed, that have the same form and no two orchestra performances that will interpret the same score in exactly the same way. Finally (and above all), epiphany within aesthetic experience is an event because it undoes itself while it emerges. This is obvious, up to the point of being banal, for lightning or for music, but I think it also holds true for our reading of literature and even for our reactions to a painting. No single meaning structure and no single impression of a rhythm pattern, for example, is ever present for more than a moment in the actual reading or listening process; and I think that, similarly, the temporality under which a painting can really "hit" us, the temporality in which we feel, for example, that it comes toward us, will always be the temporality of a moment. There is perhaps no other phenomenon that illustrates this eventness of aesthetic epiphany better than beautiful play in a team sport.[20] A beautiful play in American football and baseball, in soccer and hockey, that one element on whose fascination all expert fans can agree, independently of the victory or defeat of the team for which they are rooting, is the epiphany of a complex and embodied form. As an epiphany, a beautiful play is always an event: for we can never

predict whether or when it will emerge; if it emerges, we do not
know what it will look like (even if, retrospectively, we are able
to discover similarities with beautiful plays that we have seen before); and it undoes itself, quite literally, as it is emerging. No
single photograph could ever capture a beautiful play.

↬

For some readers at least, my *seventh* question will follow quite
naturally, after the brief reference to team sports. It is the question of whether aesthetic epiphany, the way I have now tried to
describe it, necessarily involves *an element of violence.* For other
readers, at least for those who do not watch sports, I should explain this question by specifying what exactly I mean by "violence." My question presupposes two presence-based definitions
of "power" and of "violence" that I launched in the last part of
the previous chapter. I had proposed to define "power" as the
potential of occupying or of blocking spaces with bodies, and
"violence" as the actualization of power, that is, power as performance or as event. Referring back to our discussion of the
epiphanic character of aesthetic experience, and according to the
observation that epiphany always implies the emergence of a
substance and, more specifically, the emergence of a substance
that seems to come out of nothing, we may indeed postulate that
there can be no epiphany and, as a consequence, no genuinely
aesthetic experience without a moment of violence—because
there is no aesthetic experience without epiphany, that is, without the event of substance occupying space.

But will this conclusion not inevitably provoke the politically
correct objection that by such an "aestheticization of violence,"
we are contributing to its possible legitimation? Can aesthetics
and violence go together at all? The first, obvious answer to such

a critique would be that there is a difference between labeling an act of violence as "beautiful" (this might well be a way of "aestheticizing" violence) and postulating that violence is one of the components of aesthetic experience. I am not simply saying that "violence is beautiful" (it can be beautiful, but it is not beautiful in principle), and I exclude any necessary convergence between aesthetic experience and ethical norms. Subsuming certain phenomena under the heading of "aesthetic experience" will therefore not interfere with any negative ethical judgment on their behalf. Seen from this perspective, then, my main response to the objection that I might be promoting the "aestheticization of violence" is that, by insisting on a definition of aesthetics that excludes violence, we would not only eliminate warfare, the destruction of buildings, and traffic accidents but also phenomena such as American football, boxing, or the ritual of bullfighting. Allowing the association of aesthetic experience with violence, in contrast, helps us understand why certain phenomena and events turn out to be so irresistibly fascinating for us—although we know that, at least in some of these cases, such "beauty" accompanies the destruction of lives.

Even in those forms of aesthetic experience, however, where—from a strictly physical point of view—the effect of violence is but an illusion because there is neither substance nor three-dimensional space in play (for example, when we get addicted to the "rhythm" of a prose text that we read silently,[21] or when painting "catches" our attention), we know that their effect on us can still be "violent," almost in the sense of our initial definition, that is, in the sense of occupying and thus blocking our bodies. It is surely possible to develop an addiction to a certain type of text (not only for its semantic layers) and to suffer from it; and there are certain pictures that some of us need to see over and again—however difficult and expensive this may turn out to be. After all, aesthetic experience has long been associated with welcoming the risk of losing control over oneself—at least temporarily.

       ∽

My *eighth* question has everything to do with this feeling of losing control. If there is nothing edifying in aesthetic experience, nothing positive to be learnt, *what is the effect* of getting lost in the fascination that the oscillation between presence effects and meaning effects can produce? Once we understand our desire for presence as a reaction to an everyday environment that has become so overly Cartesian during the past centuries, it makes sense to hope that aesthetic experience may help us recuperate the spatial and the bodily dimension of our existence; it makes sense to hope that aesthetic experience may give us back at least a feeling of our being-in-the-world, in the sense of being part of the physical world of things. But we should immediately add that this feeling, at least in our culture, will never have the status of a permanent conquest. Therefore, it may be more adequate to formulate, conversely, that aesthetic experience can prevent us from completely losing a feeling or a remembrance of the physical dimension in our lives.[22] Using a Heideggerian intuition once again, we can establish a categorical difference between this recuperated dimension of self-reference, the self-reference of being a part of the world of things, and that other human self-reference that has been dominant in modern Western culture, above all, in modern science: the latter is the self-image of a spectator standing in front of a world that presents itself as a picture.[23]

    Some of Federico García Lorca's poems give their readers an impression of where the opposite self-reference, that of being part of the world of things, may end up taking us.[24] In "Muerte" from *Poeta en Nueva York*, for example, Lorca makes fun of all the humans (and even of all the animals) whom he sees trying so ambitiously to be something different from what they are. Only the plaster arch, he writes at the end, is what it is—and somehow happily so: "But the plaster arch, / how vast, how invisible, how minute, / without even trying!" The existentialist thought that Lorca's poem suggests is obvious: only our death, only the moment in which we become pure matter (and nothing but matter), will truly fulfill our integration into the world of things. Only our death will give us that perfect quiet for which—sometimes in our lives at least—we long.

What this answer to the question about the effect of aesthetic experience is pointing to can also be described as an extreme degree of serenity, composure, or *Gelassenheit*. *Gelassenheit* figures as both part of the disposition with which we should open ourselves to aesthetic experience and as the existential state to which aesthetic experience can take us. In order to avoid any possible confusion of this existential state with certain hypercomplex forms of self-reflexivity (of which we intellectuals are only too fond), I have come to describe, with a deliberately colloquial formula, that specific serenity as the feeling of *being in sync with the things of the world*. What I mean by "being in sync with the things of the world" is not synonymous with a world picture of perfect (or perhaps even eternal) harmony.[25] Rather than corresponding to an ideal cosmology, the expression "in sync" refers to a situation that is very specific to our contemporary culture, that is, to the impression of having just recuperated a glimpse of what "the things of the world" might be. This may be exactly what, from an existential point of view, the self-unconcealment of Being is all about—self-unconcealment in general and not only self-unconcealment as aesthetic epiphany. Experiencing (in the sense of *Erleben*, that is, more than *Wahrnehmen* and less than *Erfahren*), experiencing the things of the world in their preconceptual thingness will reactivate a feeling for the bodily and for the spatial dimension of our existence.

Coming back to some of the classical concepts of philosophical aesthetics, we can say that unconcealment of Being may happen both in the modality of the beautiful and in the modality of the sublime; we may say that it can transport us into a state of Apollonian clarity or of Dionysian rapture. Independently of these (otherwise crucial) distinctions, I believe that we are always—deliberately or unknowingly—referring to epiphanies when, in our specific cultural situation, we use the word "aesthetic." We are referring, with this word, to epiphanies that, for moments at least, make us dream, make us long for, and make us perhaps even remember, with our bodies as well as with our minds, how good it would be to live in sync with the things of the world.

3

Now while humanists during the past two centuries have been mostly vague—and often even proud of their vagueness—whenever the question of what things of beauty might be good for came up, the practical usefulness of the study of the past has never been seriously doubted. The very concept of "history" is indeed inseparable from the promise that, once studied, the past can be "a teacher of life" (*historia magistra vitae*).[26] It is easy to show, however, how the price attached to this expectation has been growing so dramatically over the past few centuries of Western culture that, today, there is nothing more left of this expectation than some stale Sunday morning rhetoric. In the

Middle Ages, every action and every event from the past were considered to be potential orientations for the shaping of the present and the future—because the human world was not yet believed to be in permanent transformation. Therefore, every narrative about the past that people believed to be true could be turned into an "example." Renaissance culture, in contrast, would only take into account, very schematically speaking, "half of its past" for the orientation of the present. The humanists of the early modern centuries were hoping to find "examples" of relevance for their own lives in Greek and Roman antiquity— but not in the immediately preceding medieval world (which they were the first to describe as "dark"). From the late seventeenth through the eighteenth centuries, a time construction emerged that we have since come to call "historical time," and that established itself so firmly that, until recently, we tended to take it as the only possible chronotope. Historical time set the bar for "learning from the past" dramatically higher. For it implied the need to identify the "laws" that had informed historical change in the past and to extrapolate their movement into the future if one wanted to anticipate the developments to come. But even this very costly (and, as Marxists used to say, very "scientific") way of learning from the past did not survive our present-day skepticism. The latest development is not that we reject any prognostication of the future as being absolutely impossible. Rather, we anticipate it to be so complicated (and so costly) that we prefer to perform calculations of risk,[27] that is, we prefer to figure out how expensive it would be for us if certain developments that we expect to happen do not come about. Once we know the price, we can buy insurance—instead of trying to gain ultimate certainty about what the future will bring.

Another way of viewing the same development is to reevaluate the good old debate about whether our present is (still) "modern" or (already) "postmodern," which generated so much intellectual excitement only ten years ago. Today, we begin to understand that those discussions were a symptom of the chronotope of "historical time" coming to an end and that, regardless of whether we want to call our present "modern" or "postmodern," this process of exiting historical time now seems to lie behind us.[28] "Historical time" (and our concept of "history," which refers to a specific historical culture whose historicity we have only recently come to recognize) was based on the assumption of an asymmetry between the past as a "space of experience" and the future as an open "horizon of expectations." Historical time implied the assumption that things would not resist change in time but that, while the present and the future could not help being different from the past and while we were therefore constantly leaving the past behind ourselves, there was a way to "learn from the past," precisely by trying to identify "laws" of historical change and by developing, based on such "laws," possible scenarios for the future. Between that past and this future, the present appeared to be merely a short moment of transition in which humans shaped their subjectivity and used their agency by imagining and choosing among possible futures and by trying to contribute to the realization of the specific future that they had chosen. What we seem to have lost, only recently, is the self-attribution of that active movement through time ("leaving the past behind" and "entering the future") that had permeated historical time. Replacing prognostication through risk calculation, for example, means that we now experience the future as inaccessible—at least for all practical purposes. At the same time, we are more eager than ever (and better prepared, on the level of knowledge and even technology) to fill the present with artifacts from the past and reproductions based on such artifacts. Proofs are the subsequent waves of "nostalgia cultures," the unprecedented popularity and the new exhibiting styles of our museums, and the debates about the inability of societies to exist without historical memory that are so particularly intense in Europe these days. Between the "new" inaccessible future and the new past that we no longer (want to) leave behind ourselves, we have begun to feel that the present is becoming broader and that the rhythm of time is slowing down.

But what has this development (provided that mine is a plausible account of our contemporary historical culture), what has all of this to do with the concept of "presence" and its possible impact on our ways of teaching history and doing historical research? One possible answer is based on the impression that our eagerness to fill up the ever-broadening present with artifacts from the past has little, if anything to do with the traditional project of history as an academic discipline, with the project of interpreting (that is, reconceptualizing) our knowledge about the past, or with the goal of "learning from history." On the contrary, the way in which some museums organize their exhibits calls to mind the *son et lumière* shows that some historical sites in France began to offer in the late 1950s, as well as the appeal of historical novels like *The Name of the Rose* and films like *Radio Days*, *Amadeus*, or *Titanic*. All of this points to a desire for presentification—and I have certainly no objections. Short of always being able to touch, hear, and smell the past, we certainly cherish the illusion of such perceptions. This desire for presentification can be associated with the structure of a broad present where we don't feel like "leaving behind" the past anymore and where the future is blocked. Such a broad present would end up accumulating different past worlds and their artifacts in a sphere of simultaneity. Another, supplementary (rather than alternative) possibility to explain our changing relationship with the past would suggest that a new historical culture—corresponding to this new chronotope—has not yet emerged, and that a very basic (and perhaps metahistorical) level of our fascination with the past is becoming visible.[29]

If we want to better understand this basic (in the German tradition one would say "anthropological") fascination with the past, a good starting point is the phenomenological concept of the "life world." Under "life world," Edmund Husserl proposes to subsume the totality of those intellectual and mental operations that we expect all humans of all cultures and times to (be able to) perform. Historically specific "everyday worlds" can then be analyzed as multiple selections from the range of possibilities offered by the life world. One of the more astonishing features of the life world—at least from our angle of argumentation—is the general human capacity to imagine mental and intellectual operations that the human mind is *not* able to perform. In other words, it belongs to the content of our life world to imagine— and to desire—abilities that lie beyond the borders of the life world. The predicates that different cultures have given to their different gods—like omniscience, eternity, omnipresence, or almightiness—are a reservoir of such imaginations. If, based on this reflection, we claim that what we imagine to lie beyond the borders of the life world will constitute—metahistorically stable—objects of desire, we can further speculate that different desires to cross the borders of the life world in different directions may generate different basic streams of energy that will carry all historically specific cultures. The double temporal limitation of human life by birth and death, for example, will produce a desire to cross these two borders of the life world, and one half of this desire will be, more specifically, the wish to cross the border of our birth—toward the past. As an underlying force this very desire will motivate all historically specific historical cultures. The object of this desire lying under all historically specific historical cultures would be the *presentification* of the past, that is, the possibility of "speaking" to the dead or "touching" the objects of their worlds.

To say, as I have done, that such "deep" life world layers of human culture may become visible in historical moments that lie between historically specific everyday cultures—for example, between the demise of "historical time" and the emergence of a historical culture that would correspond to our broad present—by no means implies that the techniques that we develop in satisfying those basic desires—one of them being the desire for presentification—must be rudimentary. There is no reason why historical novels or historical films that provide effects of presentification should be less complex than novels and films that try to demonstrate that we can learn from history. But in which general ways are the techniques that we use in presentifying the past different, say, from the techniques of learning from the past? To judge from contemporary fascinations and practices, the techniques of presentifying the past quite obviously tend to emphasize the dimension of space—for it is only in their spatial display that we are able to have the illusion of touching objects that we associate with the past. This may explain the growing popularity of the institution of the museum and, also, a renewed interest in and reorientation of the historical subdiscipline of archeology.[30] At the same time, the trend toward spatialization makes us more aware of the limitations of historiography as a textual medium in the business of making the past present.[31] Texts and concepts certainly are the most appropriate medium for an interpretative approach to the past. But even the most basic intellectual moves of historicization seem gradually to change as soon as they begin to cater to the desire to make the past present, and such changes oblige us to revisit some basic requirements and presuppositions of the historian's profession.

The key sensitivity expected from a historian is the double capacity of, firstly, discovering objects in his own everyday worlds that have no obvious practical use in this context (that are not "ready to hand," as Heidegger would have said) and, secondly, the willingness to refrain either from finding a practical function for them or from withdrawing one's attention (leaving them as "present to hand").[32] Only this double operation of discovering objects without any practical use and refraining from finding such a use for them will produce "historical objects" and give them a specific aura—at least in the eyes of the historian and of the historically sensitive beholder. But instead of asking, at this point, what exactly such objects turned into historical objects may "mean"—which is the adequate question if we want to view them as symptoms of a past that will ultimately enable us to better understand our present—instead of asking for a meaning, presentification pushes us in a different direction. The desire for presence makes us imagine how we would have related, intellectually and with our bodies, to certain objects (rather than ask what those objects "mean") if we had encountered them in their own historical everyday worlds, Once we feel how this play of our historical imagination can be appealing and contagious, once we lure other persons into the same intellectual process, we have produced the very situation to which we are referring when we say that somebody is capable of "conjuring up the past." This is the first step toward "dealing with the things of the past," and I am quoting from the preface to the thirteenth-century Castilian

Crónica general here, "*as if they were in our own world.*" One benefit of the capacity to let ourselves, quite literally, be attracted by the past under these conditions may lie in the circumstance that, by crossing the life world threshold of our birth, we are turning away from the ever-threatening and ever-present future of our own deaths. But for our new relationship to the past, it is even more central than turning away from death that, on a general and on an institutional level, we reject the question of what benefits we might expect from engaging with the past. A good reason for leaving this question open, for letting the conjuring up of the past just happen, is that any possible answer to the question of practical benefits will limit the range of modalities through which we can indulge in the past—and simply enjoy our contact with it.

4

And what consequences, finally, could such a concentration on historical presentification and on aesthetic epiphanies have for our teaching, that is, for university teaching in the cluster of disciplines that the Anglo-American academic tradition calls the "humanities and arts"? Let me insist that the problem is not, at least not primarily, how we can accommodate that desire for presence in the classroom. What I want to discuss is whether those modified conceptions of "aesthetics" and "history," as the two main frameworks within which I propose to approach cultural objects, might—and should—have an impact on the ways we think about our teaching and go about fulfilling our pedagogical commitments. Between these two frameworks I can see a double convergence that promises to have a certain relevance for questions of pedagogy. The first such convergence is the affirmation of a marked distance from our everyday worlds, which both the happening of epiphanies and the act of historicization seem to imply and to require. Aesthetic experience imposes upon us both a situational and a temporal insularity, whereas historicization presupposes a capacity to discover and a willingness to acknowledge the dysfunctional status that certain objects of our attention have in their environments. The second convergence that I want to mention here is a double hesitation vis-à-vis our habit of interpreting, that is, of attributing meaning to, the objects of our attention. In the long run, it may be impossible for us to refrain from attributing meaning to an aesthetic epiphany or to a historical object. But in both cases (and for different reasons), I have argued that our desire for presence will be best served if we try to pause for a moment before we begin to make sense—and if we then let ourselves be caught by an oscillation where presence effects permeate the meaning effects.

As both the distance from the everyday world and the moment in which we suspend meaning attribution are conditions that we traditionally associate with aesthetics rather than with historical culture, my insistence on them may produce the impression that I want to go in the direction of an "aestheticization" of history and perhaps even of our teaching practice. But while I insist that there is nothing necessarily wrong with aestheticization, I have, on the other hand, no vested interest in it (at least not in the context of this argument).[33] What I find much more interesting is the possibility of associating the distance from everyday situations that is implied in both our conceptions of aesthetics and history with the classic—and mostly self-critical—self-reference to the academic world as an "ivory tower." For if aesthetic experience and historicization impose the distance of the ivory tower upon us, they also oblige us to acknowledge that this very distance opens up the possibility of riskful thinking,[34] that is, the possibility of thinking what cannot be thought in our everyday worlds. What cannot be thought in the everyday world are, firstly, contents, hypotheses, and options whose appearance in the everyday worlds would imply the risk of producing un-desirable consequences. For example, the question must be al-lowed in an academic discussion of whether "Martin Heidegger could have become such an important philosopher without having been so close to National Socialist ideology"[35]—but I definitely think that one should not launch this discussion on a junior high school level and probably not even in the cultural sections of the daily press. The other type of problems that can normally not be dealt with in our everyday worlds are those whose discussion promises neither solutions nor any practical yield. To concentrate on them is often considered to be too time-consuming (and therefore too costly).

If adequately understood, the ivory tower-status of the aca-demic world enables us to dwell precisely on such topics, prob-lems, and questions, without cutting off any possible feedback into society. For, to stay with the metaphor for a moment, this tower is remote from society and very different from it, but it certainly has windows and doors. That we can analyze riskful topics thanks to the tower's distance from society, and that we can work them through under conditions of low time pressure, means that, rather than being obliged to reduce their complexity (as we invariably have to do in everyday situations because we have to come up with quick solutions), we may expose ourselves to their complexity and even increase it. This is where "lived ex-perience," the second of the two convergences between our con-ception of aesthetics and our conception of history comes in. If, however, confrontation with complexity is that which makes academic teaching specific, then—instead of obsessively attrib-

uting meaning and thereby providing solutions—we should seek
to practice our teaching, as much as possible, in the modality of
lived experience (*Erleben*).[36] For good academic teaching is a
staging of complexity; it is drawing our students' attention toward complex phenomena and problems, rather than prescribing
how they have to understand certain problems and how, ultimately, they must deal with them. In other words, good academic teaching should be *deictic*, rather than interpretative and
solution-oriented. But how will such a deictic teaching style not
end in silence and, worse perhaps, in a quasi-mystical contem-
plation and admiration of so much complexity? For an analogy
that helps to clarify this point, we can turn to the—emphatic—
new concept of "reading" that probably comes from the specific
experience that readers have had with certain types of modern
literature. Such "reading," both reading books and reading the
world, is not simply meaning attribution. It is the never-ending
movement, the both joyful and painful movement between losing and regaining intellectual control and orientation—that can
occur in the confrontation with (almost?) any cultural object as
long as it occurs under conditions of low time pressure, that is,
with no "solution" or "answer" immediately expected. This is
exactly the movement that we are referring to when we say that a
class or a seminar "broadened" our minds.

Almost inadvertently (but by no means randomly), in this
discussion of the consequences that a presence-oriented conception of aesthetics and of history may imply for our teaching, we
have arrived in the intellectual vicinity of some of the classical
authors on the subject of academic teaching and the academic
institution. Niklas Luhmann, for example, used to characterize
the university as a "secondary social system," that is, as a social
system whose function should be the production of complex-

and in channeling them into a conversation among the students, and with the students that goes further than any individual reaction to complexity could have possibly gone. At the same time, the other key task of the teacher must be to keep these debates close to their objects of reference (mostly texts, of course), not to let them take off into boundless and uncoordinated speculation. However difficult it may be to describe this process with some precision, everybody who has ever attended a good university will know what I am talking about and what kind of pedagogical gift I am alluding to. It is the gift, above all, of remaining alert and absolutely open to the others, without falling into the trap of becoming absorbed by their intuitions and positions, and it is the gift of intellectual good taste that stays focused on those very topics that do not allow for quick and easy solutions. Such openness and such focus define the teacher as a catalyst of intellectual events—and I associate the function of the catalyst with the condition of physical presence. It is not completely unthinkable, of course, that such an event-driven, open-ended conversation, "emerging toward an unknown goal," might be organized in an electronic medium—for example, in a chat room (although chat rooms have not yet achieved simultaneous writing and reading, and their name does not seem to promise much intellectual excitement).[42] But we know from experience, at least from the experience of contemporary generations of media users, that discussions under these conditions are hardly ever as intense and as productive as even an average conversation will be in real presence.[43] Why exactly this is so and whether it has to remain like this forever are, of course, questions open to speculation.

Personally and for the time being, I am certainly determined to offer some resistance (in the quiet form of inertia) to the furor of replacing every bit of real-presence interaction that is left with those deplorably hygienic computer screens. Other than that, it seems almost inevitable (although it somehow feels strange) that I should conclude this chapter by saying that it was perhaps necessary to go through such a relatively complicated development of the concept of "presence" in order to realize that our own teaching profession, very specifically and in not yet completely thought through ways, has always been about real presence. But there is no guarantee that this will continue. The future of presence needs our present commitment.

To Be Quiet for a Moment:
About Redemption

1

"I can see how you are fascinated by the concept—but what do you really get out of 'presence'?" a friend asked me when I was on the final stretch of the previous chapter.[1] Struggling with the pages about the possible future of academic teaching, I told him, with the guarded friendliness of a corporate answering machine, that what he was bringing up was exactly one of my big points, that a reflection on presence would show how hopeless it was for the humanities to try and justify their existence by pointing to some "social function" or "political yield." This was not, however, what my friend had wanted to know, as I understood from his reaction, which also showed me that he had not intended his words to be a mildly aggressive rhetorical question. Could it be all about me, specifically and, so to speak, existentially about me, not just about my book and the world? It was, I assume (and fear), about me—about me as my friend's obnoxiously verbal senior colleague who cannot refrain from reading any text he sees (including, for example, do-it-yourself instructions for gadgets that I have no interest in), and it was about me as the unbearable pop psychologist who cannot help interpreting every tiny movement on the faces of the people he is talking to. It was about a fifty-five-year-old professor of literature who would be lonesome and probably without an income in this world were it not for the strange (and relatively recent) development in Western culture that has promoted enthusiasm for the reading of literature into a possible professional career. But what interest—or what problem—could it then have been that got me, of all people (and, one might even add, of all academics), to profess that that culture at large, including literature, was not only about meaning, that even in the teaching of literature and culture we should pause, from time to time, and be silent (for presence cannot use too many words)?

Surprisingly, at least for a member of the famously self-reflexive (and loquacious) guild of the humanists, my friend's personal question caught me by surprise and, being a typical humanist, I immediately followed the impulse and started thinking about what I really get out of presence[2]—for I did not want to miss this welcome opportunity to find out (even) more things about myself. At first, I retrieved only memories—potentially depressing memories—from those years when we all believed in the healing powers of psychoanalysis. Hadn't that amazing wisdom once been revealed to my self, while the bodily container of that self was sitting (not lying!) on a couch, that all those humans who, like myself, had a reputation of being workaholics were working so much and trying so hard out of an intense (albeit vague) fear simply of being lazy in their ultimate essence and reality? And is it not true that I have a tenaciously and pleasantly recurrent daydream about my existence after retirement as a state of just "being there,"[3] that is, as a life form that would simply occupy space without doing much else? I also felt that I suddenly understood why that one particular stanza by Federico García Lorca[4] had always impressed me so much, in which the poet makes fun of all those humans (and even of those animals) who constantly strive to excel themselves whereas, as Lorca writes in the last line, "that plaster arch is so great because it just quietly is what it is." Suggestions (with all kinds of incentives) that I surpass, transform, and even "rejuvenate" myself (but why would I want to be young?) come incessantly from my professional world and from my social environments, and I admit that I am a bit tired of them, perhaps because they resonate with the half-conscious, long-accumulated conviction that I have never been (nor ever will be) "good enough" anyway.

But in the process of growing older (or, from a Californian perspective, "more mature"), I have learnt to appreciate the repetitiveness of those everyday rituals with no crescendo that—if one only wants to—are easy to protect against any interference, like the family dinner on workdays; and as I grow even more mature, I am also beginning to discover how I often wish, in retrospect, that some conversation had been "a perfect conversation," or that some day had been "a perfect day." Now I know that I shall never allow myself to call a day "a perfect day" without having the certainty that what was good about it for me had conquered my body—up to the point indeed of giving me the feeling that I was, somehow, the embodiment of that perfect day. If this sentence looks strange and dangerously tautological, I can offer, as an alternative description, my impression that it is, primarily, this very feeling of being the embodiment of something that I am referring to when I speak, often with too much emphasis and emotion, about *presence*. A perfect day, I think, may well appear perfect, at least in retrospect, because it was filled, the way a lake is progressively filled by the movement of a wave, by that one, and in itself short, moment of intense joy that hit me, *including my body*, at some point—but the perfect day can, of course, also be made of that one moment of intense sadness, of a black sadness that sinks into my organs. For Denis Diderot, in contrast, a perfect day was a day when he and his friends joined in the freedom of "letting things be," when any pleasure and any temporary occupation (ranging from political discussions to attending to one's makeup) were possible, joyful, and present—because none of these occupations had a purpose.[5] I suspect that what lies behind my fixation on the form and the substance of the "perfect day" is a longing—disappointment of which is ultimately, needless to say, for the better—for those moments of intensity to last, which, of course, they never will.

Short of ever letting myself be convinced that a day was a homogeneously perfect day indeed, I have come to accept that an alternation between intensity and perfect quietness would probably be good enough.[6] Perhaps this is just like daytime and nighttime. One can certainly trigger and even buy intensity. The problem (the asymmetry) is that while I know that such intensity will at some point become exhausting (or even boring), the quietness never comes without me wishing it to last longer, if not forever. At the end of most of my days, I am already eager to wake up early enough for some intellectual agitation—but I also wish that I could, literally, sleep forever. This may well be a death wish—but I think it is above all the opposite. For could Heidegger's *Gelassenheit* not mean being simultaneously quiet and wide-awake? Perhaps there is not all that much of an opposition between being fully agitated and being fully quiet. The (famous) "wish to be a tree" perhaps (and even the wish to be a plaster arch) are not only death wishes. For is *Gelassenheit* not also the perfect state of presence? The intensity of wanting to be and of being there, unpermeated by effects of distance. Such moments could be the origin of the tension between presence and meaning that has been a leitmotif for my book. I constantly fear that effects of meaning (at least an overdose of them) might diminish my moments of presence—but I know, at the same time, that presence could never become perfect if meaning was excluded. For while meaning perhaps never does emerge without producing effects of distance, it is also true that I could not be "there" in the full sense of my existence, if meaning were completely out of the question.

Every attempt to describe "what I get out of presence" seems to lure me into this slightly embarrassing staccato of juxtaposing concepts that do not easily go together. So let me change the thrust of my question and ask, "How could one get there?" rather than "What is presence?" And as soon as I ask, "How can I get there?"— to the intense quietness of presence—the word "redemption" comes to mind. But redemption would not only be, as in some romantic and theological versions of the concept, a return to a primordial state whose innocence has been lost by reason of some "original sin." The redemption that I imagine would be a return—and more. I imagine redemption as a state to be reached through the paradox of ecstasy,[7] that is, by pushing an initial relationship, a given situation of distance, to an extreme degree of eccentricity and even of frenzy, in the hope of achieving a union—or, even better, a presence-in-the-world— that at first seemed to be as much out of reach as any other dream. How could we get there? Perhaps by singling out, preferably on that perfect day, strong individual feelings of joy or of sadness—and by concentrating on them, with our bodies and our minds; by letting them push the distance between us (the subject) and the world (the object) up to a point where the distance may suddenly turn into an unmediated state of being-in-the-world.

2

But if I exclude recourse to a logic of individual sin and redemption, "Redemption from what?" becomes the secondary question through which the initial question ("What do I get out of presence?") reconnects with the social dimension. It could be redemption from the permanent obligation to move and to change, both in the sense of the never-ending "historical" changes imposed upon us, on all different levels of our existence, and in that of the self-imposed obligation that makes us want constantly to "surpass" and transform ourselves. Feeling that such permanent movement originates outside ourselves, we have, at least since the early twentieth century, tended to attribute its dynamic to "society." Jean-François Lyotard once called the feeling of having to follow the rhythms of those mostly intransitive—and often vehement—movements a *mobilisation générale*.[8] Our work today leaves us more free time than any previous generation had, and yet none of us ever has enough time. No doubt, it is our being caught in such general mobilization that makes us long for—and appreciate so much—those short moments of concentration on "the things of the world" and the intense quietness that comes with it.

The problem may then be, as Georges Bataille put it, writing about the (culturally determined) relationship that we (do not) entertain with our bodies, that our distance from such concentration and quietness may have grown to a point where we run the risk of no longer even missing what we have lost.[9] But would we not also have to say—to admit?—that today we are experiencing a stage beyond that point of—seemingly—absolute loss, a stage where, paradoxically, the desire for what we had absolutely lost is coming back? A stage where, strangely enough, this lost desire is even being imposed "back" upon us? For contemporary communication technologies have doubtlessly come close to fulfilling the dream of omnipresence, which is the dream of making lived experience independent of the locations that our bodies occupy in space (and in this sense, it is a "Cartesian" dream). Our eyes can see, in real time, how a river on another continent is swelling to a flood, how an athlete, ten thousand miles away, is running faster than any other human being before him ran, and we indulge in "watching" warfare at prime time, without any danger to our bodies. Sometimes, we sit at a dinner table with our friends and talk to our children who have stayed at home. We remain "available"—and being "available" is being "generally mobilized"—for business calls while we are on a date. But if watching a war that is an ocean and a continent away from us can definitely repress even the thought of what a war means to those who are physically close to it, if the floating images on the screens that are our world may become a barrier that separates us forever from the things of the world, those same screens may also reawaken a fear of and a desire for the substantial reality we have lost.[10] Clearly, our reactions can go either way. The strange logic that I am interested in and that I am trying to point to, however, seems to go like this: the more we approach the fulfillment of our dreams of omnipresence and the more definite the subsequent loss of our bodies and of the spatial dimension in our existence seems to be, the greater the possibility becomes of reigniting the desire that attracts us to the things of the world and wraps us into their space.[11]

This, by the way, is the surprisingly complex (and mostly overlooked) content of the concept "special effects" (and "special effects" are just a part of what I call "effects of presence" in the preceding chapters). At their very best—or, more precisely, at their most efficient (which means with a little luck, because our reactions, as I said before, can always go in the opposite direction, that is, in the direction of forgetting)—at their very best, contemporary communication technologies, paradoxically, may bring back what has become so "special" because it has been excluded by the very environment that consists of the accumulation and coupling of gadgets.[12] In this sense, it is probably—at least we may hope so—not all that important to try and recuperate a media-induced feeling of what it must be like to be on a sinking ocean liner in the North Atlantic. But it matters, I think, to expose oneself to special effects that reproduce the impact of an air raid—and also (although we hardly ever call such moments "special effects") to allow oneself to be touched, literally, by the intensity of a voice that comes from a compact disk or by the closeness of a beautiful face on a screen.

This is not exclusively an effect of the technology involved. It also has to do with our habit of concentrating more on the faces that we see in a film or on the screen than on the faces of those with whom we sit at a table or to whom we make love—a "bad habit" no doubt, yet better than a complete oblivion of closeness. So I am trying to neither condemn nor give a mysterious aura to our media environment. It has alienated us from the things of the world and their present—but at the same time, it has the potential for bringing back some of the things of the world to us. And if it became clear again that sitting together at a table for dinner (or making love, for that matter) is *not only about communication*, not only about "exchange of information," then it might indeed become important and helpful—not only for some romantic intellectuals—to have *concepts that would allow us to point to what is irreversibly nonconceptual in our lives*.

Sometimes I wonder whether our predominant epistemologies, our everyday epistemologies and our academic epistemologies, do not affect us within a logic similar to that of special effects. Given where the trajectory of Western thought has led us, given also the devastating political impact, during the past few centuries, of philosophies and ideologies based on ontological premises and on claims to absolute truth, we may indeed have no real alternative—for most practical purposes—to the range of worldviews that we subsume under names like "constructivism" or "pragmatism."[13] But inhabiting worlds (and the plural is of the essence here) that we want to be shaped and "constructed" by changing sets of concepts, discourses, and narratives obviously produces a desire for what these concepts, discourses, and narratives—at least when seen from a constructivist or pragmatic perspective—no longer even pretend to touch. And perhaps that desire, too, becomes stronger the more perfectly constructivist we are. For many young (and not so young) people, piercing their bodies is a way of feeling "grounded," of giving themselves a—somehow ontic—certainty of being "alive."[14] My point is not, of course, that we should therefore simply return to a more "substantialist" way of thinking and living, although I do believe that "we humanists," of all people, should have the time to take this desire seriously and to do something with it. Much would be gained, I believe, if such reactions at least allowed us to be quiet for a moment from time to time amid the technological and epistemological noise of our general mobilization. Procrastination will not be a threat: for we find ourselves in an environment that will not let us pause for more than *moments of presence*.

3

I hope it has become clear by now that this short book was by no means intended to be a "pamphlet against" concepts and meaning at large, or against understanding and interpretation. Neither is it written against the Cartesian legacy of our contemporary culture(s). Simply finding the words to describe such potential misunderstandings immediately makes it clear how absurd—how grotesque and even how "fascist"—it would be to renounce concepts, meaning, understanding, or interpretation. My marginal (but I hope not completely trivial) contribution is, rather, to say that this Cartesian dimension does not cover (and should never cover) the full complexity of our existence, although we are led to believe that it does with probably more overwhelming pressure than ever before.

But somehow I must have produced the misunderstanding that I was dreaming of the dark world of pure substance,[15] and this impression has provoked some of the most powerful criticisms of my work over the past few years. In general, I want to say that I would agree with each of these criticisms if my proposal were indeed to simply replace what I call "our Cartesian legacy." All I am saying, however, is that we should take the time to think about and to react to some consequences that the *exclusive* dominance of the Cartesian worldview has produced—and it is a widespread confusion to assume that thinking about something implies an imperative to change or even to replace it.[16] In this spirit, then, I concede that what I have to say in this book does not comply with the general expectation that our work in the humanities will be "critical" in a political or (less specifically) in a "social" sense.[17] I am—at least mildly—critical, I believe, as far as the loss of the presence-dimension in contemporary culture is concerned. But it is true—and I want to stress this—that there is something "affirmative" in my argument. Being critical always implies one agenda of transformation or another (and there is nothing wrong with that!), whereas a concentration on the things of the world rather comes with the desire to be "quiet for a moment" (which I don't find reprehensible either). If some friends, colleagues, and readers (particularly of my own generation) want to interpret this wish to be quiet as a move toward being conservative (or even as a "betrayal" of some generational legacy)—I cannot help it. I might even feel a sense of solidarity with the ecological politicians who have been accused (both absurdly and with good reason) of being "neoconservative." Above all, however, I would like to ask in return: Why should one feel an obligation toward the blind spots of one's own generation?

In the previous chapter, I have reacted to the interpretation that reads the desire to "be in sync with the things of the world" as a desire for harmony—which, of course, converges with the allegation that my position is not "critical" enough or even (God forbid!) "affirmative." In principle, I can see two motivations behind this judgment. Its background can be either a general prejudice against whatever may be harmonious or the fear that giving in to a wish for harmony may divert our attention from a "reality" that is nothing less than harmonious. I admit that I cannot sympathize with the first objection (although it is, of course, easy to imagine the aesthetics of a world that would exclude harmony). But accepting the full and awe-inspiring responsibility of representing the worldview of an aging man, I insist that—as an aging man indeed—I have come to treasure the rare moments of harmony that happen to me. So much so that I believe we should never let our political commitments (if we have any) completely obscure this longing. For what, after all, would be the point of politics and potential transformations without a vision of a more enjoyable life?

More aggressive is the question whether there is not a pathology—the pathology of "fetishism"—behind the desire to be in sync with the things of the world.[18] I certainly cannot see an affinity between what I am arguing for and the meaning that Karl Marx has given to this word. Under fetishism, he criticizes an attachment to the "physical" aspects of commodities, a fixation that makes us unable to understand these commodities as the symptom and expression of social relations, more specifically as the symptom and expression of the specifically capitalistic "conditions of economic production."[19] If I must react specifically to this meaning of the word "fetishism," then I shall have to insist, once again, that I am really not interested in a radical repression of the dimension of meaning—to which an understanding of the conditions of production would belong. On a more general level, I should probably add that the desire for presence and thingness that I want to promote is not at all synonymous with a desire to "possess" or only to "hold on" to these things. Rather, I want to insist on what might be recuperated by simply (and ever so lightly) reconnecting with the things of the world—and being sensitive to the ways in which my body relates to a landscape (while I am hiking, for example) or to the presence of other bodies (while I am dancing) is certainly not equivalent to the desire of possessing real estate or to daydreams of sexual dominance. In the Freudian tradition, the concept of fetishism highlights an individual's fixation on certain (types of) objects, a fixation and an addiction that cannot be explained by any conscious interest that individuals have in these objects. The one critical question that derives from the Freudian use of the concept is, then, whether the desire of being in sync with the things of the world necessarily implies the risk of producing an addiction, that is, whether it can obliterate our capacity of ever standing at a distance from the things of the world. One response has to be, again, that being more sensitive to the things of the world in general is not synonymous with being fixated on *specific* things. Above all, however, I would like to ask back whether the concern with fetishism does not imply a—problematic—fixation on intellectual (and even on spatial) "distance" as an absolute value.

4

For all of the self-irony and intellectual distance that I have tried so hard to apply to the intellectual "agenda" of my generation, the so-called "generation of 1968," with its by now grotesque commitment to eternal youth and its sometimes masochistic fixation on an exclusively "critical" worldview; for all my eagerness to avoid a fetishistic attachment to the values of that never-ending intellectual adolescence, there has been one "generational" reaction to my thoughts about "presence" that really caught me by surprise—so much so, indeed, that it finally triggered some very generation-specific concerns.[20] I am talking of the suspicion (or was it rather meant to sound like praise?) that I had turned into a "religious thinker."[21] Whatever the intention behind that interpretation may have been, it hit me almost as hard as an insult—which I found quite strange from the beginning.

My first line of argument was therefore purely defensive—and I now know that this was too simple-minded. But how could somebody who, far from experiencing any attacks of guilt about it, does not even feel good about not going to church, I replied, how could such an average renegade and his book be labeled as "religious" if they didn't make a single reference to a god or to a transcendental sphere that such a god might inhabit? Was my desire to reconnect with the things of the world not as strictly immanentist as one could possibly imagine? Indeed, my friends

said, this desire for the things of the world is so strictly immanentist that it appears to have a mystical touch (or more than
just a touch thereof). After all, I was longing for a greater closeness to the things of the world and for a greater intensity in this
contact than our everyday worlds would allow for—and in this
literal sense, my desire was certainly "transcendental." More than
slightly embarrassed by the lack of a powerful counterargument,
I asked myself, very seriously for the first time, whether it was
possible that I had turned into a "religious thinker" without
knowing and without wanting it. So I rediscovered a fascination
with theology that goes back to my first years at the university—
and that I now think never completely vanished. And had those
intellectuals who—in the name of the Enlightenment tradition—tried to exclude theology from the academic world not always looked very narrow-minded and even pathetic to me? Were
they not the seven dwarfs of Enlightenment, whose overindustri-
ous disposition was turning a grand intellectual legacy into a
sweaty middle-class ideology?

Whether I felt more encouraged or more defeated when I subsequently discovered a strong affinity with the work of a contemporary group of young British theologians whose position
has been described as "radical orthodoxy," I cannot remember.
But "to rescue ontology from the sole dominance of epistemology" was certainly a project to my taste, a project that I could
identify with. Even more so with a self-description of radical orthodoxy provided by Catherine Pickstock, according to which
"political ethics [should] cease to be reactive and [should] accord
primacy to the projects of the human imagination that combine
appearing bodies and do not just futilely acknowledge invisible
subjects."[22] Was this, the suggestion "to combine appearing

bodies," not exactly what I was longing for? Would such a concentration on appearance not help us to build a world where we
could be more than "invisible subjects"?

(Un)fortunately, however (unfortunately for my sympathy
and fortunately for reasons of conceptual clarity), I found myself
on the side that Pickstock characterizes as "the more subtly idol-
atrous hypostasisation of the unknown 'beyond being'" in her
next paragraph, a paragraph that I shall quote in its entirety because—accepting the place that I assume is assigned to positions
like my own—it contains an illuminating answer to the question
of where the border between religious thinking and nonreligious
thinking may run. Pickstock calls "theology" what I am referring
to as "religious thinking,"[23] and the quotation starts with her attempt to describe practices that acknowledge the existence of
limits put on human control and rationality, although they
would never define themselves as "religious" or "theological":

> But equally we could retain suspicion of these projects as only par-
> tially and inadequately displaying what we can never fully com-
> mand, while also acknowledging that that mystery was somewhat
> present in human beings never reducible to players in civic proc-
> esses. The secular equivalent of both grace and *via negativa* would
> in this way think beyond either the idolatry of the humanly insti-
> tuted, or the more subtly idolatrous hypostatization of the un-
> known "beyond being." It would rather conceive the appearance of
> the withheld or the withholding within appearance. This thought
> also requires the liturgical practice of searching to receive as a mys-
> tery from an unknown source that grace which binds human beings
> together in harmony. But to think such a thing is to think theologi-
> cally; the "secular equivalent" fades into the thinking of incarnation
> and deification, and the search for a liturgical practice that would
> allow for the continuous arrival of the divine glory to humanity.[24]

I am certainly not claiming that Catherine Pickstock is wrong in any aspect of her complex argument, or that this argument and her entire position should not be taken seriously (either at the university or in any other intellectual context). All I want to say is that, for the time being, I simply do not resonate with her description of "liturgical practice" as "searching to receive as a mystery from an unknown source that grace which binds human beings together in harmony." My reasons must be personal and existential—for I cannot associate them with any potential flaws in the intellectual position of "radical orthodoxy." For the time being, then, Pickstock's description simultaneously separates me from "religious thinking" and shows why the impression of an intellectual closeness to religious thinking is certainly appropriate.

Not without polemical intention, I suppose, Pickstock writes "being" (in the sense of *Sein*) with a lowercase "b" in the sentence where she indirectly refers to Heidegger. "Being"—written with a capital "B"—must look, from her perspective, like an attempt to be simultaneously theological and nontheological. This brings up the question of whether it is possible and legitimate to think of something "beyond" those beings (lowercase "b") or entities that make up our everyday worlds—*without becoming theological?* Pickstock's answer to this question must be "no." It is my conviction, in contrast, that "Being," understood as "the things of the world devoid of any conceptual grid," is a concept that neither implies nor requires (nor excludes!) a reference to the "liturgical practice" that in Pickstock's language marks the border between "theological thought" and "subtle idolatry." The border, of course, remains open—and I am not saying this because I feel like getting ready to cross that line (I am indeed mildly shocked by how indifferent I feel about it). But it is true that, different from the concept of "Being" in and by itself, the late Heidegger's perspectives on a "history of Being," and on the possibility or impossibility of an "unconcealment of Being" occurring, clearly lie on the theological side. For he speaks of the alternation between situations where the unconcealment of Being is possible and others where it becomes unlikely, as a movement completely out of the reach of human thinking and knowledge and therefore, at least potentially, as "a mystery from an unknown source."[25] In the end, everything may depend on whether one feels disposed (or even pressed) to ask questions about this "unknown source," whether one perhaps even has the desire to be in contact or communication with it. There are no explicit texts, to my knowledge, that oblige us to assume that Heidegger had this desire—for all the implicit theological motifs in his philosophy. So I find myself, once again, much closer to Heidegger than I would like to be (if I had a choice).

5

In the final pages of this book, I shall try to describe the marvelously quieting effect that some productions of No and Kabuki, the classical staging forms of Japanese theater, have had on me—independently of any intellectual concerns that I was aware of. This is why I shall resist, as best I can, the temptation to explain, once again,[26] my ideas about a possible relationship between these staging forms and Zen Buddhism, and between Zen Buddhism and Heidegger's concept of Being. For I really believe that there is nothing more intellectually kitsch than the enthusiasm for Zen Buddhism among Western intellectuals who (like myself) do not know a single Asian language and have, at best, a touristic knowledge of one or other Asian culture. I would simply note here that Zen understands "nothingness" as a dimen-

sion where things are not shaped by forms and concepts, and
therefore as a sphere that is withdrawn from the grasp of human
experience (and this is the opinion of recognized experts).[27] Zen
masters teach their disciples to resist the temptation of thinking
the transition of the unshaped from nothingness into what a
certain Western tradition would call the "everyday world," that
is, into a world structured by concepts and forms. For if the unshaped ever crossed this border, it would have to adopt forms.

Without any claim to expertise, then, I would like to suggest
that we can associate a certain stage device that is central to No
and Kabuki with the one thought that Zen does not allow its
disciples to think.[28] In No and Kabuki, all the actors come to the
stage and leave the stage across a bridge that leads from a
"house" (a wooden container large enough for the bodies of several actors) through the audience to the stage (the seats that are
close to the middle of this bridge are the most expensive). Now,
this emerging and vanishing of the theatrical personae often
takes up more time than the actual scenes and interactions in
which the actors participate on the stage. Synchronized, in No
theater, with the (for Western ears) monotonous beat of two
types of archaic drums, the actors' bodies seem to gain form and
presence as they come forth from behind a curtain and approach
the stage in an almost endlessly protracted sequence of forward
and backward movements. When they withdraw from the stage,
the actors once again perform a similar choreography, now producing the impression that they are undoing their forms and
their presence. No pieces, in particular, and their music are
breathtakingly slow and repetitive. But if you overcome the first
impulse that is likely to come up in a Western spectator, if you
resist the wish to leave the theater after the first half hour or so, if
you have enough patience to let the slowness of emerging and

vanishing of form and unformed presence grow on you, then, after three or four hours, No can make you realize how your rapport to the things of the world has changed. Perhaps you even begin to feel the composure that allows you to let things come, and perhaps you cease to ask what these things mean—because they seem just present and meaningful. Perhaps you even observe how, while you ever so slowly begin to let things emerge, you become a part of them.

But is this not, finally, a religious experience—or, to say the least, the surrogate of a religious experience? Under my (I have to insist: precarious) impression that No drama and Kabuki drama look like the Zen motif of an impossible transition from nothingness into the world of forms and concepts, it is actually possible to find an answer to this question, an answer, however, that is as ambiguous as the demons are, those souls of the deceased who come back to the world and haunt the living. Demons seem to take even more time than the other characters to reach the stage in Kabuki and No. Once they arrive at the stage, they can adopt all kinds and forms of human bodies and human roles. But when they are supposed to be "just demons," the actors do whatever they can to blur any impression of formedness. Then their hair looks wild, the rhythms of their body movements seem to grow more irregular, and in the Kabuki pieces (where the actors do not wear masks), their eyes are neither closed nor open, and their tongues are sticking out. For the demons are of this world—and not of it. Their presence on the stage ends up producing moments of silent intensity, that is, moments of extreme quietness and of extreme excitement. The demons' tongues are flesh but, being part of these strange characters' ontic ambiguity, they are also words and language.

As the rhythms and the appearances of Japanese theatre were

conquering my body and my imagination, I remembered the Pentecostal tongues from the Christian tradition. I also remembered those faces with their suddenly blurred forms and their half-open eyes that we all see at some special and very rare moments of our lives: sweet faces and threatening faces indeed. Threatening and sweet, religious and not, I do not want to miss any of those faces. In this book, I have done my intellectual best to conjure them up, and in future I shall try to stay as close to them as I possibly can.

Reference Matter

Notes

Materialities/Nonhermeneutic/Presence

1. Essays originating in these colloquia were published in the following volumes: Bernard Cerquiglini and Hans Ulrich Gumbrecht, eds., *Der Diskurs der Literatur- und Sprachhistorie: Wissenschaftsgeschichte als Innovationsvorgabe* (Frankfurt a/M, 1983); Hans Ulrich Gumbrecht and Ursula Link-Heer, eds., *Epochenschwellen und Epochenstrukturen im Diskurs der Literatur- und Sprachhistorie* (Frankfurt a/M, 1986); Hans Ulrich Gumbrecht and K. Ludwig Pfeiffer, eds., *Stil—Geschichten und Funktionen eines kulturwissenschaftlichen Diskurselements* (Frankfurt a/M, 1986); Hans Ulrich Gumbrecht and K. Ludwig Pfeiffer, eds., *Materialität der Kommunikation* (Frankfurt a/M, 1988); Hans Ulrich Gumbrecht and K. Ludwig Pfeiffer, eds., *Paradoxien, Dissonanzen, Zusammenbrüche: Situationen offener Epistemologie* (Frankfurt a/M, 1991). A selection of essays from the final two volumes is available in English translation as Hans Ulrich Gumbrecht and K. Ludwig Pfeiffer, eds., *Materialities of Communication*, trans. William Whobrey (Stanford, 1994).

2. See Friedrich Kittler, *Discourse Networks 1800/1900* (Stanford, 1990), the original German version of which, *Aufschreibesysteme 1800/1900*, appeared in 1985 (David Wellbery's brilliant introduction to the

English translation by Michael Metteer and Chris Cullens draws a complex picture of the intellectual environment of Kittler's book, which was also the environment of the Dubrovnik colloquia); Paul Zumthor, *Introduction à la poésie orale* (Paris, 1983), id.*: La Lettre et la voix: De la "littérature" médiévale* (Paris, 1987); *Les Immatériaux: Épreuves d'écriture. Ouvrage publié à l'occasion de la manifestation Les Immatériaux* (Centre national d'art et de culture Georges Pompidou) (Paris, 1985); Jacques Derrida, *La Voix et le phénomène* (Paris, 1967) (on the exteriority of the signifier in Derrida's work, see David Wellbery, "The Exteriority of Writing," *Stanford Literature Review* 9.1 [1992]: 11–24); Niklas Luhmann, *Social Systems* (Stanford, 1995).

3. See Hans Ulrich Gumbrecht and K. Ludwig Pfeiffer, eds., *Schrift* (Munich, 1993), partly translated into English in *Stanford Literature Review* 9.1 and 9.2 (1992).

4. Since I wrote the first draft of this chapter, I have been reminded to my great embarrassment that it is my (former student) friend and now eminent colleague João Cézar de Castro Rocha who deserves the credit for this breakthrough intuition. I refrain, however, from offering the obvious (Freudian) interpretation of my memory's initial refusal to render João's name.

5. This is how the author—not without mixed feelings—explains to himself the beginning of his fascination with Heidegger's philosophy, especially his antimetaphysical arguments. See Martin Heidegger, *Sein und Zeit* (1927), 15th ed. (Tübingen, 1984), §§18–24, for Heidegger's critique of Descartes and the elimination of the spatial dimension in his philosophy.

6. See Hans Ulrich Gumbrecht, "Rhythm and Meaning," in *Materialities of Communication*, pp. 170–82.

Metaphysics: A Brief Prehistory of What Is Now Changing

1. Joshua Landy proposed that I should say "hypophysics" rather than "metaphysics," given the latter term's strongly religious connotation. But although it is true that this connotation differs from the way

I use the word here, I decided not to make the change, because however trivial the traditional "critique of metaphysics" may be (another friend recently suggested that it might be one of the forgotten entries in Flaubert's *Dictionnaire des idées reçues*), what I try to develop here is inevitably part of this very tradition in Western philosophy.

2. For the history of "interpreting things" and the philosophical problems implied, see Miguel Tamen, *Friends of Interpretable Objects* (Cambridge, Mass., 2001).

3. See Hans Ulrich Gumbrecht, "Ausdruck," in Karlheinz Barck, Martin Fontius, Dieter Schlenstedt, and Burkart Steinwachs, eds., *Ästhetische Grundbegriffe* (Stuttgart, 2000), 1: 416–31. For more general reference, see also Hans Ulrich Gumbrecht, "Sign-Concepts in Everyday Culture from the Renaissance to the Early Nineteenth Century," in R. Posner, K. Robering, and T. A. Sebeok, eds., *Semiotics: A Handbook on the Sign-Theoretic Foundations of Nature and Culture* (New York, 1998), pp. 1407–27. I apologize for chiefly citing my own publications in the notes to this chapter. But as I want to keep its historical argument succinct and clearly geared toward the "theoretical" issues at stake, it is impossible to present a detailed, well-documented narrative and a thorough analysis of all the historical periods and phenomena in question. At the same time, however, I felt obliged to give at least some evidence of being familiar with these materials.

4. I am not clear about how much of a convention it was, during the Middle Ages, to call the principles of medieval Bible interpretation "hermeneutics."

5. Here I discuss what ended up being the result of a long and complicated conceptual transition, in which multiple positions emerged that were neither as "clearly Protestant" nor as "clearly Catholic" as my presentation seems to suggest, as a contrast between two different theological interpretations of the Eucharist.

6. See Hans Ulrich Gumbrecht, "Für eine Erfindung des mittelalterlichen Theaters aus der Perspektive der frühen Neuzeit," in Johannes Janota et al., eds., *Festschrift Walter Haug und Burghart Wachinger* (Tübingen, 1992), 1: 827–48.

7. See Rainer Warning, *Funktion und Struktur: Ambivalenzen des geistlichen Spiels* (Munich, 1974), pp. 215–17.

8. There is a tradition in cultural history and the history of philosophy, however, of using Descartes's name with this negative connotation. It is quite telling, for example, that in *Being and Time,* in his first coherent attempt at reformulating the subject/object paradigm, Heidegger uses atypically aggressive language to criticize Descartes (not just Cartesianism!) for the exclusion of the dimension of space from his philosophy (the very dimension that constitutes itself around the human body). See esp. § 21.

9. For a panoramic view, based on contributions by eminent specialists in this field, see Hans Ulrich Gumbrecht, Rolf Reichardt, and Thomas Schleich, eds., *Sozialgeschichte der Aufklärung in Frankreich*, 2 vols. (Munich, 1984).

10. See Robert Darnton, *The Business of Enlightenment: A Publishing History of the "Encyclopédie," 1775–1800* (Cambridge, Mass., 1979).

11. Michel Foucault, *Les Mots et les choses: Une Archéologie des sciences humaines* (Paris, 1966), pp. 221–24. Translated as *The Order of Things: An Archaeology of the Human Sciences* (New York, 1970).

12. See Hans Ulrich Gumbrecht, *Eine Geschichte der spanischen Literatur* (Frankfurt a/M, 1991), pp. 580–93.

13. For the meanings of this word during the eighteenth and early nineteenth centuries, see Hans Ulrich Gumbrecht and Rolf Reichardt, "Who Were the *Philosophes*?" in Gumbrecht, *Making Sense in Life and Literature*, trans. Glen Burns (Minneapolis, 1992), pp. 133–77.

14. Foucault, *Les Mots et les choses*. On Luhmann's work on the observer concept and its historical context, see Niklas Luhmann, Humberto Maturana, Mikio Namiki, Volker Redder, and Francisco Varela, *Beobachter: Konvergenz der Erkenntnistheorien?* (Munich, 1900).

15. See Hans Ulrich Gumbrecht and Jürgen E. Müller, "Sinnbildung als Sicherung der Lebenswelt—Ein Beispiel zur funktionsgeschichtlichen Situierung der realistischen Literatur am Beispiel von

Balzacs Erzählung 'La Bourse,'" in Hans Ulrich Gumbrecht, Karlheinz Stierle, and Rainer Warning, eds., *Honoré de Balzac* (Munich, 1980), pp. 339–89.

16. See Hans Ulrich Gumbrecht, *Zola im historischen Kontext: Für eine neue Lektüre des Rougon-Macquart-Zyklus* (Munich, 1978).

17. See Hans Ulrich Gumbrecht, "Struggling Bergson: An Eight-Step Attempt at a Frame Narrative for the *Fin de siècle*," in Andreas Kablitz et al., eds., *Das Imaginäre des Fin de siècle* (Freiburg, 2002), pp. 65–82.

18. For the following, see Bernhard Siegert, "Das Leben zählt nicht: Natur- und Geisteswissenschaften bei Dilthey aus mediengeschichtlicher Sicht," in Claus Pias, ed., *Medien. Dreizehn Vorträge zur Medienkultur* (Weimar, 1999), pp. 161–82.

19. I am, of course, referring to Peter Berger and Thomas Luckmann, *The Social Construction of Reality* (New York, 1966).

20. See, e.g., I. A. Richards, *Science and Poetry* (London, 1926).

21. In literary studies, nobody has articulated and (if one may say so) argued this complaint more efficiently than Paul de Man.

22. See Hans Ulrich Gumbrecht, "About Antonin Artaud and the Miseries of Transgressing," in Gerhard Neumann and Rainer Warning, eds., *Transgressionen: Literatur als Ethnographie* (Freiburg, 2003), pp. 315–32.

23. See Ferdinand Fellmann, *Phänomenologie und Expressionismus* (Freiburg, 1982), pp. 57–61. A detailed historical analysis of the main philosophical motifs of the conservative revolution can be found in the final chapter of my book *In 1926: Living at the Edge of Time* (Cambridge, Mass., 1997), pp. 437–78.

24. Not by coincidence, the German word *Dasein,* which Heidegger uses for "human existence," contains the spatio-deictic syllable "da." See n. 8 above.

25. See, as an emblematic book for the German version of "immanente Interpretation," Wolfgang Kayser, *Das sprachliche Kunstwerk: Eine Einführung in die Literaturwissenschaft* (Bern, 1948).

26. As a terminus post quem for this first wave of epistemological "hardening," we can point to the publication of Claude Lévi-Strauss's *Anthropologie structurale* (Paris, 1958).

27. See Hans Ulrich Gumbrecht, "Déconstruction Deconstructed: Transformationen französischer Logozentrismuskritik in der amerikanischen Literaturwissenschaft," *Philosophische Rundschau* 33 (1986): 1–35; H. Aram Veeser, ed., *The New Historicism* (New York, 1989), and Hayden White, *Metahistory: The Historical Imagination in Nineteenth-Century Europe* (Baltimore, 1973).

28. The importance of Friedrich Kittler's work lies in the possibility of reading it as a move of compensation in this context. Besides his *Discourse Networks 1800/1900*, see also the highly programmatic collective volume edited by Kittler, *Austreibung des Geistes aus den Geisteswissenschaften: Programme des Poststrukturalismus* (Paderborn, 1980).

Beyond Meaning: Positions and Concepts in Motion

1. Jacques Derrida, *Of Grammatology*, trans. Gayatri Chakravorty Spivak, rev. ed. (Baltimore, 1997), p. 14.

2. For an essay written under the spell of similar soft terrorism, see Hans Ulrich Gumbrecht: "Who Is Afraid of Deconstruction?" in Harro Müller and Jürgen Fohrmann, eds., *Diskurstheorien und Literaturwissenschaft* (Frankfurt a/M, 1987), pp. 95–114.

3. Gianni Vattimo, *Beyond Interpretation: The Meaning of Hermeneutics for Philosophy* (Stanford, 1997).

4. Ibid., p. 27. This, of course, is the place to mention the notorious episode called "Sokal's Hoax," which cautioned many humanists against a hermeneutic overconfidence; see my commentary, "Blinde Überzeugungen: Wie Sokals Jux erst moralisiert und dann zerredet wurde. Über das Verhältnis von politischem Bekenntnis und wissenschaftlicher Forschung," *Die Zeit*, February 28, 1997. For a more serious (and ultimately no less efficient) position than Sokal's, see Steve Chu, "The Epistemology of Physics," in Heidrun Krieger Olinto and Karl Erik Schollhammer, eds., *Novas epistemologias: Desafios para a universidade do futuro* (Rio de Janeiro, 1999), pp. 13–32. Chu, one of

the 1997 Nobel laureates in physics, is far from giving up facticity claims, being well aware of science's interpretative dimension.

5. Vattimo, *Beyond Interpretation,* p. 13.

6. Umberto Eco, *The Limits of Interpretation* (Bloomington, Ind., 1990), pp. 6f.

7. Jean-Luc Nancy, *The Birth to Presence,* trans. Brian Holmes et al. (Stanford, 1993), p. 6.

8. Ibid., pp. 4f.

9. Karl Heinz Bohrer, *Ästhetische Negativität* (Munich, 2002), p. 7.

10. Ibid., p. 310.

11. George Steiner, *Real Presences* (1986; pbk. ed., Chicago, 1989).

12. Ibid., p. 4.

13. Everything would depend, in such a discussion, on a narrower or wider definition of "theology" and "religion." This at least was my impression after a discussion with David Wellbery at a colloquium in Rio de Janeiro in 1998, when he insisted on the (for him unavoidably) theological basis of my (then relatively vague) thoughts on "production of presence."

14. Steiner, *Real Presences,* p. 227.

15. Ibid., p. 215.

16. In a discussion that we had in May 2002, Nico Pethes remarked that this capacity of substance/materiality to be energized is different from (if not opposite to) the function of substance/materiality in serving as a "support" for the storage of information and knowledge, and I agree.

17. Judith Butler, *Bodies That Matter: On the Discursive Limits of "Sex"* (New York, 1993), p. 9. Butler took this stance after having embraced positions that can be characterized as constructivist in her earlier work.

18. Ibid., p. 10.

19. Michael Taussig, *Mimesis and Alterity: A Particular History of the Senses* (New York, 1993), p. xvi.

20. Ibid., pp. xviiif.

21. Martin Seel, *Ästhetik des Erscheinens* (Munich, 2000).

22. Hans-Georg Gadamer, *Hermeneutik, Ästhetik, Praktische Philosophie*, ed. Carsten Dutt, 3d ed. (Heidelberg, 2000), p. 63.

23. See Martin Heidegger, "The Origin of the Work of Art," in id., *Poetry, Language, Thought*, ed. and trans. Albert Hofstadter (New York, 1971), pp. 15–88, esp. pp. 41f.

24. Heidegger, *Sein und Zeit*, 15th ed. (Tübingen, 1984), p. 11 (my emphasis).

25. For the details of this quick historical contextualization, see Gumbrecht, *In 1926*, pp. 437–78.

26. Heidegger, *Sein und Zeit*, §§ 20 and 21, pp. 92–101.

27. See esp. § 23, pp. 104–10.

28. If it is not inappropriate to do so, I would like to dedicate the following Heidegger commentary—in fond intellectual opposition—to my colleague Thomas Sheehan.

29. See, e.g., Heidegger, "Origin of the Work of Art," p. 56: "Truth happens in the temple's standing where it is"; "Thus in the work it is truth, not only something true, that is at work."

30. Ibid., pp. 39f.

31. Martin Heidegger, "Der Ursprung des Kunstwerkes," in *Holzwege*, 7th ed. (Frankfurt a/M, 1994), pp. 1–74, here p. 25: "Die Kunstwerke zeigen durchgängig, wenn auch in ganz verschiedener Weise, das Dinghafte" (see also pp. 11f.).

32. Martin Heidegger, *Introduction to Metaphysics*, trans. Gregory Fried and Richard Polt (New Haven, Conn., 2000), p. 42.

33. Ibid., p. 142.

34. Ibid., pp. 194f.

35. Martin Heidegger, "Zur Erörterung der Gelassenheit: Aus einem Feldweggespräch über das Denken," in *Gelassenheit*, 10th ed. (Pfullingen, 1992), pp. 27–71; quotation from pp. 40f. I am translating Heidegger's enigmatic conceptual invention *Gegnet*—which is central to this text—with "clearing of Being."

36. In trying to answer this question, I refer to my essay "Martin Heidegger and His Japanese Interlocutors: About a Limit of Western Metaphysics," *Diacritics* 30.4 (Winter 2000): 83–101.

37. In ibid., I base this additional assumption, above all, on the strong affinity that Heidegger felt with Asian thought, especially with Zen Buddhism.

38. Catherine Pickstock drew my attention to this aspect.

39. See Heidegger, "Zur Erörterung der Gelassenheit," p. 33.

40. On the philosophical and historical dimensions of this distinction, see Heidegger, "Die Zeit des Weltbildes," in id., *Holzwege,* pp. 75–114.

41. Heidegger, "Zur Erörterung des Gelassenheit," p. 57 (see also p. 44).

42. Heidegger never replaces the concept of the "work of art" with "aesthetic experience" (a substitution that has become almost obligatory today), no doubt because "aesthetic experience" is semantically close to the dimension of consciousness and therefore easy to associate with the phenomenological dimension.

43. Heidegger, "Origin of the Work of Art," p. 71.

44. Ibid., p. 41.

45. Ibid., p. 48.

46. Ibid., p. 42.

47. Ibid., p. 42.

48. Seel, *Ästhetik des Erscheinens,* pp. 31–33, opts for this second interpretation.

49. p. 49.

50. p. 43.

51. See Glenn W. Most, "Heideggers Griechen," *Merkur* 634 (2002): 113–23.

52. See, for an earlier version of the same typology, "Ten Brief Reflections on Institutions and Re/Presentation," in Gert Melville, ed., *Institutionalität und Symbolisierung: Verstetigungen kultureller Ordnungsmuster in Vergangenheit und Gegenwart* (Cologne, 2001), pp. 69–75.

53. See my article: "Fiktion/Nichtfiktion," in H. Brackert and E. Lämmert, eds., *Funkkolleg Literatur,* vol. 1 (Frankfurt a/M, 1977), pp. 188–209.

54. See Mikhail Bakhtin, *Rabelais and His World* (Cambridge, Mass., 1968).

55. This exactly is the point that I failed to make, many years ago and on behalf of the rhetorical trope of the hyperbole in medieval texts, in my doctoral dissertation, Funktionswandel und Rezeption: Studien zur Hyperbolik in literarischen Texten des romanischen Mittelalters (Munich, 1972).

56. What follows in the final pages of this chapter has previously been formulated in "Four Ways to See (or Bite) a Body in a Text," Internet Diskussionsforum des Romanischen Seminars der CAU Kiel, ed. J. Dünne, A. Arndt, and U. Rathmann, Impulstext Wintersemester 1998/99 (http://ikarus.pclab-phil.uni-kiel.de/romanist/IDF-FRAM.htm).

57. See my "Wie sinnlich kann Geschmack (in der Literatur) sein? Über den historischen Ort von Marcel Prousts *Recherche*," in Volker Kapp, ed., *Marcel Proust: Geschmack und Neigung* (Tübingen, 1989), pp. 97–110, and "Eat Your Fragment!" in Glenn Most, ed., *Collecting Fragments / Fragmente sammeln* (Göttingen, 1997), pp. 315–27.

58. For historical examples of such behavior, see Miguel Tamen's chapter on iconoclasm in id., *Friends of Interpretable Objects,* pp. 28–49.

59. See my "Ausdruck," in Karlheinz Barck, Martin Fontius, Dieter Schlenstedt, Burkhart Steinwachs, and Friedrich Wolfzettel, eds., *Ästhetische Grundbegriffe,* vol. 1 (Stuttgart, 2000), pp. 416–31.

Epiphany/Presentification/Deixis: Futures for the Humanities and Arts

1. *American Heritage Dictionary of the English Language*, 4th ed. (Boston, 2000), s.v. "futures."

2. See my "The Consequences of an Aesthetics of Reception: A Deferred Overture," an essay first published in German in 1975 and reprinted in translation in Gumbrecht, *Making Sense in Life and Literature,* pp. 14–29.

3. See Karl Heinz Bohrer, "Die Negativität des Poetischen und das

Positive der Institutionen" (Stanford Presidential Lecture, 1998), *Merkur* 598 (1999): 1–14.

4. I am reacting here to a discussion with Ursula Link-Heer, who argues that Heidegger's epistemological interest in what I am referring to as aesthetic experience must lead, of necessity, to an "apotheosis" of literature and art. My double response is that (a) Heidegger never explicitly claimed, to my knowledge, any exclusive epistemological status for the work of art, and that (b), even if he had done so, it should be possible to use some of his concepts without following him in this.

5. With respect to historicization, I refer to my *In 1926*. As regards pedagogy, see my "Live Your Experience and Be Untimely! What 'Classical Philology as a Profession' Could (Have) Become," in Glenn W. Most, ed., *Disciplining Classics / Altertumswissenschaft als Beruf* (Göttingen, 2002), 253–69, a revised version of which appeared as the final chapter of my *The Powers of Philology: Dynamics of Textual Scholarship* (Champaign, Ill., 2003).

6. The title of the course that we ended up teaching (twice) during the fall quarters of the academic years 2000/2001 and 2001/2002 was "Things of Beauty," and the paradigms for aesthetic experience that we dealt with were Mozart's *Don Giovanni*, the glass and steel architecture of the Crystal Palace, García Lorca's collection of poems *Poeta en Nueva York*, athletic beauty (exemplified through footage from the 1936 Olympics), and paintings by Jackson Pollock and Edward Hopper.

7. This was the central thesis of Franz Koppe's book *Sprache und Bedürfnis. Zur sprachphilosophischen Grundlage der Geisteswissenschaften* (Stuttgart, 1977). I disagree, however, with Koppes's proposal that "making us aware of situations of collective need" should be considered as the main and genuine function of aesthetic experience (Koppe, by the way, speaks of "*Vergegenwärtigung* von Bedürfnissituationen," but he does not understand *Vergegenwärtigung* in the sense that I try to give to the word "presentification").

8. From this point on, I shall use the phrase "aesthetic experience"

only in the sense of *ästhetisches Erleben* although—for purely stylistic reasons—I shall mostly skip the word "lived" in "lived experience."

9. See Bohrer, "Negativität des Poetischen und das Positive der Institutionen." Bohrer has never completely severed ethical norms from aesthetic experience, however: see his "Das Ethische am Ästhetischen," *Merkur* 620 (2000): 1149–62.

10. I derive this concept from Alfred Schuetz and Thomas Luckmann, *Strukturen der Lebenswelt* (Neuwied, 1975), pp. 190–93.

11. The allusion to Heidegger's notion of *Gelassenheit* ("composure," "serenity") is deliberate. *Gelassenheit* is mentioned here as an attitude that can facilitate the happening of aesthetic experience as a moment of intensity; I shall return to the concept when I try to describe the possible effects of aesthetic experience on our psyches.

12. See Hans Ulrich Gumbrecht, Ted Leland, Rick Schavone, and Jeffrey Schnapp, "The Athlete's Body Lost and Found," preface to *The Athlete's Body, Stanford Humanities Review* 6.2 (1998): vii–xii.

13. Nancy, *Birth to Presence*, p. 6.

14. Gadamer, *Hermeneutik, Ästhetik, Praktische Philosophie.*

15. Niklas Luhmann, *Die Kunst der Gesellschaft* (Frankfurt a/M, 1995), esp. pp. 30f. and 41.

16. See my essay "Die Stimmen von Argentiniens Leichen," *Merkur* 499 (1990): 715–28.

17. This is one of the aspects where my own reflection on aesthetic experience comes the very closest to Seel's *Ästhetik des Erscheinens.*

18. Heidegger, "Origin of the Work of Art," p. 71 (emphasis in original).

19. Ibid., p. 42 (emphasis in original).

20. See Hans Ulrich Gumbrecht, "On the Beauty of Team Sports," *New Literary History* 30 (Spring 1999): 351–72, and id., "A forma da violencia: Em louvor da beleza atlética," in *Mais!* cultural supplement to *Folha de São Paulo*, March 11, 2001, the basis for a short book on athletic beauty entitled *Lob des Sports* (Frankfurt a/M, forthcoming).

21. Regarding the violent impact that the rhythm in a printed text can have on its readers, see Hans Ulrich Gumbrecht, "Louis-Ferdi-

nand Céline und die Frage, ob literarische Prosa gewaltsam sein kann," in Rolf Grimminger, ed., *Kunst Macht Gewalt: Der ästhetische Ort der Aggressivität* (Munich, 2000), pp. 127–42.

22. Georges Bataille was addicted to this structure of argumentation. See "L'Apprenti Sorcier," in Denis Hollier, ed., *Le Collège de sociologie (1937–1979)* (Paris, 1979), pp. 36–59, esp. pp. 40, 59.

23. Martin Heidegger, "The Age of the World Picture," in id., *The Question Concerning Technology and Other Essays* (New York, 1977), pp. 115–54.

24. See Hans Ulrich Gumbrecht, "Präsenz. Gelassenheit: Über Federico García Lorcas 'Poeta en Nueva York' und die Schwierigkeit, heute eine Ästhetik zu denken," *Merkur* 594–95 (1998): 808–25.

25. I am reacting here to a discussion with my colleague Hermann Dötsch.

26. Reinhart Koselleck traces the rise and the decline of this promise since the late seventeenth century in "Historia magistra vitae: Über die Auflösung des Topos im Horizont neuzeitlich bewegter Geschichte," in *Vergangene Zukunft zur Semantik geschichtlicher Zeiten* (Frankfurt a/M, 1979), pp. 38–67.

27. See Niklas Luhmann, *Observations on Modernity* (Stanford, 1998), pp. 44–62.

28. My argumentation here strongly relies on the work of Reinhart Koselleck. See his books in English translation: *Future's Past* (Cambridge, Mass., 1991) and *The Practice of Conceptual History: Timing History, Spacing Concepts* (Stanford, 2002). For my own attempts to further develop Koselleck's thought, see Hans Ulrich Gumbrecht, "Die Gegenwart wird (immer) breiter," *Merkur* 629–30 (2001): 769–84; "Space Reemerging: Five Short Reflections on the Concepts 'Postmodernity' and 'Globalization,'" in Hermann Herlinghaus, ed., *Postmodernidad y globalización* (Pittsburgh, 2003); and, above all, the chapter "After Learning from History," in Gumbrecht, *In 1926*.

29. For a more detailed version of the following argument, see "Historical Representation and Life World," pt. 2 of Gumbrecht, *Making Sense in Life and Literature,* pp. 33–75.

30. See Mike Pearson and Michael Shanks, eds., *Theater/Archeology* (New York, 2001); the concept of "theater" stands for the spatial dimension of relating to the past.

31. In this spirit, my book *In 1926* was meant to be an experiment in the identification of such limits.

32. See Hans Ulrich Gumbrecht, "Take a Step Back—and Turn Away from Death! On the Moves of Historicization," in Glenn Most, ed., *Historicization/Historisierung* (Göttingen, 2001), pp. 365–75.

33. Hans Georg Gadamer, *Wahrheit und Methode* (Tübingen, 1961), p. 142, suggests that there is a systematic relationship between aesthetics and the dimension or *Erleben* ("lived experience")—which dimension, in the phenomenological tradition, corresponds to the interval between (physical) perception and experience as meaning attribution.

34. For this concept, see Hans Ulrich Gumbrecht, "Riskantes Denken. Intellektuelle als Katalysatoren von Komplexität," in Uwe Justus Wenzel, ed., *Der kritische Blick: Intellektuelle Tätigkeiten und Tugenden* (Frankfurt a/M, 2002), pp. 140–47.

35. This was a question asked by Jacques Derrida at a seminar at the University of Siegen (Germany) in 1988.

36. For a more extended discussion of this aspect, see Hans Ulrich Gumbrecht, "Live Your Experience—and Be Untimely! What 'Classical Philology as a Profession' Could (Have) Become," in Glenn Most, ed., *Disciplining Classics / Altertumswissenschaft als Beruf* (Göttingen, 2002), pp. 253–69. The specific concept of *Erleben* that I try to promote here (in full awareness of a widely shared prejudice against it in contemporary philosophy) is *not* Wilhelm Dilthey's concept of *Erleben*, in the sense of a "retranslation of objectivations of life into that spiritual liveliness from which they emerged." As mentioned earlier, I use *Erleben* to refer to the interval between the physical perception of an object and the (definitive) attribution of a meaning to it; unlike Dilthey, I am not recommending that the reading of a poem, for example, should bring us back to the poet's (lived) experience that first motivated it.

37. See Niklas Luhmann, *Die Wissenschaft der Gesellschaft* (Frankfurt a/M, 1990).

38. Max Weber, *Wissenschaft als Beruf* (1919; Munich, 1921). See my detailed analysis of Weber's text in "Live Your Experience," pp. 253–60.

39. Wilhelm von Humboldt, "Über die innere und äußere Organisation der höheren wissenschaftlichen Anstalten in Berlin," in id., *Studienausgabe,* vol. 2, ed. Kurt Müller-Vollmer (Frankfurt a/M, 1971), pp. 133–41.

40. This was also the prediction of the former Stanford President, Gerhard Casper, in "Eine Welt ohne Universitäten?" (Werner Heisenberg Vorlesung, Munich, July 3, 1996), whose line of argumentation I follow in the final section of this chapter.

41. See Gumbrecht, "Live Your Experience," p. 263.

42. I borrow the concept of "emerging toward an unknown goal" from Martin Seel.

43. See, for the documentation of an early—and hardly encouraging—experiment of this kind, the electronic conversation among French intellectual luminaries in *Les Immatériaux.*

To Be Quiet for a Moment:
About Redemption

1. This friend was, again, Joshua Landy, without whose demanding encouragement I would indeed have abandoned the project of this book. Disappointed readers should therefore turn to him with their complaints.

2. The question of what I really get out of presence obviously became the beginning of this chapter. If one could individually dedicate chapters of books that are already otherwise dedicated in their entirety, I would dedicate this one to Robert Harrison, who at some point was honest enough to tell me that he had hoped that I would write a "more poetic book" than what these pages are now turning into. I fear they will frustrate his expectations. For these pages may only show what a

good thing it is that I otherwise—very carefully and completely—
repress my poetic drives.

3. Yes, I am alluding to Peter Sellers's film under this title.

4. Federico García Lorca, "Muerte," in id., *Poeta en Nueva York*
(México, D.F., 1940).

5. I owe this Diderot reference to Henning Ritter. Diderot's perfect day was September 15, 1760, and he described it in a letter to his
friend Sophie Volland.

6. The attempt to think presence as the synthesis of opposites goes
back to a question by Werner Hamacher. After a lecture in which I
tried to describe the presence effects of aesthetic epiphanies, he asked
me what the "dark side of the moon" would be in my concept of presence.

7. See P. Heinrich s.v. "Ekstase," in Joachim Ritter, ed., *Histori-
sches Wörterbuch der Philosophie* (Basel, 1972), 2: 434–36.

8. See Jean-François Lyotard, *The Inhuman: Reflections on Time*
(Stanford, 1991), esp. pp. 58–77.

9. See Georges Bataille, "L'Absence de besoin plus malheureuse
que l'absence de satisfaction," in Denis Hollier, ed., *Le Collège de sociologie* (Paris, 1979), pp. 38f.

10. About the screens that are our world, see Wlad Godzich, "Language, Images, and the Postmodern Predicament," in Hans Ulrich
Gumbrecht and Karl Ludwig Pfeiffer, eds., *Materialities of Communication* (Stanford, 1994), pp. 355–70.

11. For further examples exemplifying this "logic," see my essay
"nachMODERNE ZEITENraeume," in Robert Weimann and Hans
Ulrich Gumbrecht, eds., *Postmoderne—globale Differenz* (Frankfurt
a/M, 1991), pp. 54–70.

12. I refer here to the discussions of the Stanford Presidential Colloquium on Engineering and the Humanities about "special effects"
that took place in February 2000.

13. My main reference here is the philosophical work of Richard
Rorty, to whose political importance I fully subscribe.

14. This thesis about the psychic benefits of piercing goes back to a letter from (and empirical observer experience of) Thomas Schleich.

15. Which words remind me of Friedrich Kittler's *Die Nacht der Substanz* (Bern, 1989).

16. This is, I think, what Heidegger meant when he highlighted that thinking always implies an aspect of "in die Acht nehmen." See Martin Heidegger, *Was heißt Denken?* (1954), 4th ed. (Tübingen, 1984), version 2, lecture 8, p. 124.

17. I am reacting here to another important objection made by Werner Hamacher.

18. Here I am referring back to a discussion with my friend Luiz Costa Lima in a seminar that I taught at Rio de Janeiro in May 2002.

19. Karl Marx, *Das Kapital*, pt. 1, "Ware und Geld," in id. and Friedrich Engels, *Werke* (Berlin, 1983), 23: 86f.

20. Why "generational" asks Trina Marmarelli—and may well be on target with her implicit criticism. I, in contrast, thought that the question had to be typical in a generation for whose large majority any type of commitment to religion is—or at least used to be—categorically out of the question.

21. I first heard it in 1998, as an expression of concern, I guess, from David Wellbery. But the same suspicion also belongs to the list of incessant criticisms that Joshua Landy has kept me alert with (see the first footnote of chapter 2).

22. Catherine Pickstock, "Postmodern Scholasticism: A Critique of Recent Postmodern Invocations of Univocity" (MS, Cambridge, 2002), p. 38.

23. Yet another question (a question much debated, today, in the intellectual world of "religious studies" and one to which Charlotte Fonrobert drew my attention) is whether "theology" is indeed the equivalent of "religious thinking." For my own purposes in the context of this book, however, I don't think that the distinction between "religious thinking" and "theology" would make a difference.

24. Pickstock, "Postmodern Scholasticism," p. 38.

25. Not by coincidence, Heidegger's famous sentence "only a God can help us," from the posthumous *Spiegel* interview, occurs in a context where he talks about history of Being.

26. See Hans Ulrich Gumbrecht, "Martin Heidegger's Japanese Interlocutors: About a Limit of Western Metaphysics," *Diacritics* 30.4 (Winter 2000): 83–101.

27. See, e.g., Keji Nishitani, *Religion and Nothingness* (Berkeley, 1982).

28. Karl Ludwig Pfeiffer's very impressive descriptions of Japanese theater were a strong initial reason to expose myself to the experience of No and Kabuki: see Pfeiffer's *The Protoliterary: Steps Toward an Anthropology of Culture* (Stanford, 2002), pp. 131–34, 143–66.

Index

aesthetic experience, 94, 163n42, 165n4, 165n7, 166n17; as oscillation between presence effects and meaning effects, 2, 104–11; and epiphany, 94, 111–13; and ethics, 94, 102, 166n9; and presence, 95; and teaching, 96–97, 165n6; extended field of, 97, 165n6; specificity of, 99–101; insularity of, 101–3, 126; and composure, 103–4, 116–18, 166n11; and violence, 114–16; as *ästhetisches Erleben*, 165–66n8. *See also* aesthetics

aesthetics, 118; and presence, 20; eighteenth-century emergence of, 37; Seel's treatment of, 63; and contemporary Western philosophy, 72; relationship to history and pedagogy, 93–96, 125–28; and ethics, 102; and lived experience, 168n33. *See also* aesthetic experience

"Against Interpretation" (Sontag), 10

Anthropologie structurale (Lévi-Strauss), 160n26

Aristotle, 18, 65. *See also* sign, Aristotelian concept of

Artaud, Antonin, 46

arts, as academic discipline: xv, 91, 93, 95–96, 98, 101, 125. *See also* humanities

Ästhetik des Erscheinens (Seel), 63, 166n17

Aufschreibesysteme 1800/1900 (Kittler), 8–9, 160n28

"À une passante" (Baudelaire), 103

Bakhtin, Mikhail, 85, 102

Barck, Karl Heinz, 6

Bataille, Georges, 46, 138, 167n22

Baudelaire, Charles, "À une passante," 103

Being, Heidegger's notion of: 53; and presence, 19, 66–67, 77, 78, 81; and truth, 47, 67–73; history of, 55–56, 70, 172n25; movement of, 68–69; and things of the world, 70; and *Dasein*, 71; and work of art, 72–74; relationship to Heidegger's "earth" and "world," 74–77; unconcealment of, 117–18; Pickstock's treatment of, 147–48; and Zen Buddhism, 149; and

45; and presence, 59, 64, 109; and
epiphany, 113; teaching of, 134
lived experience (*Erleben*), 43, 100,
107, 127–28, 166n8, 168n33, 168n36
Lorca, Federico García, 98, 116–17;
"Muerte," 117, 134–35; *Poeta en
Nueva York*, 117, 165n6
Luhmann, Niklas, 10, 38, 107, 128–
29
Lyotard, Jean-François, 9–10, 138

Machiavelli, Niccolò, 27, 89
Mallarmé, Stéphane, "Un coup de
dés," 41
Marmarelli, Trina, 171n20
Marxism, xv, 7, 8, 46, 48. See also
Marx, Karl
Marx, Karl, 144. *See also* Marxism
Materialität der Kommunikation
(conference proceedings), 7
"Materialities of Communication"
(conference), 8, 9
materiality: of communication, 6–9,
11, 13, 15–18, 49, 92; and meaning,
12; of world, 25; of signifier, 30,
40–41; of objects of aesthetic
experience, 59, 109, 161n16; of
body, 60–61; and culture, 62
meaning: and presence, xiv, 19, 57–
59, 63, 77, 105–11, 124, 134, 136–37;
identification of, 1–2, 13, 16, 21,
25, 26, 54; production of, 8, 16,
64; structures of, 9, 13, 14, 16; and
materiality, 11–12, 16; emergence
of, 13, 15, 49; and communication,
16; in poetry, 18; of objects, in
Middle Ages, 25–26; replacement
of substance by, in Protestant theology, 29–31; in classical French
theater, 32–33; destabilization of,
41, 52; and Being, 68, 77; absurd-
ity of renouncing, 142, 144. *See
also* Cartesian worldview; herme-

neutic field; hermeneutics; interpretation; subject-object paradigm
meaning cultures, 19, 79–87, 89, 106
meaning effects, xv, 2, 18, 19, 49,
107–11, 116
metaphysics, xiv; history of Western,
22–49; and deconstruction, 51–53;
ontological duplicity of, 110; as
"hypophysics," 156–57n1; critique
of, 156–57n1
Molière, 32
moments of intensity, 97–99, 100–
101, 101–2, 111, 113, 135–36, 151,
166n11
Morales, Pablo, 104
Mots et les choses, Les (Foucault), 37,
38
Mozart, Wolfgang Amadeus, 97, 99;
Don Giovanni, 165n6
"Muerte" (Lorca), 117, 134–35

Nancy, Jean-Luc, 111; *The Birth to
Presence*, 57–58, 105–6
new criticism, 45, 48
new historicism, 48
Nietzsche, Friedrich, 41–42, 86
nonhermeneutic field, 14–16, 18, 65,
93

object, xiii–xiv, 8; history of human
relationship with, 25–27, 36, 38–
39, 42, 45, 72; and Being, 68–69;
elements of meaning and presence
in, 79; of aesthetic experience, 97,
100–105, 107–9, 111, 125–26, 128;
historical, 120–24, 125–26, 128;
and fetishism, 144
observer, first-order, 27, 38–39; second-order, 3, 38–40
Of Grammatology (Derrida), 51
ontology: Cartesian, 17, 33, 81; and
Encyclopédie, 36; and Heidegger,
65, 78, 112; and epistemology, 146